PRAISE FOR NICKI MINAJ

"It was only a matter of time before a hip-hop star would blow through the lines separating pop from rap and appeal to two lucrative audiences at once. And it was as inevitable that hip-hop purists would swiftly cry foul. It is particularly upsetting to the hip-hop boys club that the most successful transgressor, a freshly minted megastar named Nicki Minaj, is a woman."

—Brent Staples, The New York Times

"She's proud to be shameless, with the hooks to back it up."

—Robert Christigau, MSN Music

"At her best, Nicki Minaj is, line for line, one of the wittiest, most creative rappers working today, either male or female. Her many personas and voices fly through her songs with joyful abandon, and she seems to be having so much fun astonishing us. On the first half of her second album, "Pink Friday ... Roman Reloaded," the Trinidadian American rapper from New York City offers repeated evidence of her talents, and she delivers funny, biting, bawdy lines and rhyming couplets with apparent glee."

—Los Angeles Times

"Nicki Minaj, she's definitely one of the great ones…you know how we recognized LeBron [James] was a great one, Tiger [Woods] was a great one, and Kobe [Bryant] was a great one? Nicki is up there. Her story has just begun."

—Diddy, MTV News

Nicki Minaj:

The Woman Who Stole The World

AN UNAUTHORIZED BIOGRAPHY

Nicki Minaj:

The Woman Who Stole The World

AN UNAUTHORIZED BIOGRAPHY

Lynette Holloway

Colossus Books
An Imprint of Amber Communications Group, Inc.
Phoenix
New York   Los Angeles

Nicki Minaj: The Woman Who Stole the World

Published by:
Colossus Books
An Imprint of Amber Communications Group Inc
1334 East Chandler Boulevard, Suite 5-D67
Phoenix, AZ 85048
E-mail: AMBERBK@aol.com
WWW.AMBERBOOKS.COM

Tony Rose, Publisher/Editorial Director
Yvonne Rose, Associate Publisher
The Printed Page, Interior/Cover Design

Colossus Books are available at special discounts for bulk purchases, sales promotions, fund raising or educational purposes. For details, contact: Special Sales Department, Amber Books, 1334 E. Chandler Boulevard, Suite 5-D67, Phoenix, AZ 85048, USA.

Copyright © 2012 by Lynette Holloway and Amber Communications Group, Inc.

Paperback ISBN # 978-1-937269-30-2
EBOOK ISBN # 978-1-937269-31-9

Library of Congress Cataloging-in-Publication Data

Holloway, Lynette.
  Nicki Minaj : the woman who stole the world : an unauthorized biography / Lynette Holloway.
      pages cm
  Includes bibliographical references and index.
  ISBN 978-1-937269-30-2 (alk. paper)
  1. Minaj, Nicki. 2. Rap musicians--United States--Biography. 3. Hip-hop--United States. I. Title.
  ML420.M518H65 2012
  782.421649092--dc23
  [B]
                          2012030948

Dedication

To my mother, thanks for being my guiding light.

Acknowledgements

First and foremost I'd like to thank God. I'd also like to thank Tony and Yvonne Rose of Amber Communications Group, Inc. for a wonderful opportunity. I'd also like to offer a heartfelt thank-you to my HB, family and friends. Thank you all!

Contents

Dedication   vii

Acknowledgements   ix

Introduction—Nicki Minaj –The Modern Queen of Hip Hop   1
    "A Moment for Life"   2

I. Nicki Minaj Growing Up   5

II. Lil Wayne Signs Nicki Minaj   9
    Nicki and Friends Photo Journey   13
    "I'm the Best"   20

III. Behind The Making of the first album-"Pink Friday"   23
    "Blazin"   27

IV. Nicki's Launch Toward Superstardom   29
    "Fly"   32

V. Nicki Minaj: Fashion Icon   35
    Nicki Minaj: Fashion Icon Photo Journey   41
    "Roman's Holiday"   50

VI. Grammy Awards Ceremony   53
    "Roman Reloaded"   56

VII. The Making of Pink Friday: Roman Reloaded   59
    "Starships"   66

VIII. Nicki Minaj on Tour: Starships, Superbowl and Scandal   67
    Roman Reloaded 2012 Tour Dates   76
    "Did it on Em"   78

IX. BET, Boobs and the Bronx   79
   "Pound the Alarm"   90

X. Nicki Minaj Tops the Charts   91

Conclusion   97

Studio Albums/Singles   100

About the Author   103

Nicki Minaj—The Modern Queen of Hip-Hop

The only question for Nicki Minaj is how far she wants to take the game. She has littered the landscape with past MCs like Lil Kim and Foxy Brown, who for all intents and purposes have been outcast by this futuristic Barbie.

—Lynette Holloway

A Moment For Life

I fly with the stars in the skies,
I am no longer trying to survive,
I believe that life is a prize, but to live doesn't mean you're alive.

Don't worry bout me, and who I fire
I get what I desire, it's my empire
And yes I call the shots, I am the umpire
I sprinkle holy water, upon the vampire (vampire)
In this very moment I'm king,
In this very moment I slay Goliath with a sling,
This very moment I bring
Put it on everything, that I will retire with the ring

And I will retire with the crown, Yes!
No I'm not lucky I'm blessed, Yes!
Clap for the heavyweight champ, Me!
But I couldn't do it all alone, We!

Young Money raised me, grew up out in Baisley
Southside Jamaica, Queens and it's crazy
cause I'm still hood, Hollywood couldn't change me
shout out to my haters, sorry that you couldn't face me
ain't being cocky we just vindicated, best believe that when
*   we done*

This moment will be syndicated, I don't know, this night just
*   remind me of everything that they deprived me of, pppp-*
*   put ya drinks up, it's a celebration every time we link up*
We done did everything they can think of
Greatness is what we on the brink of.
[Chorus]
I wish that I could have this moment for life, for life, for
*   life Cuz in this moment I just feel so alive, alive, alive*

I wish that I could have this moment for life, for life, for life Cuz in this moment I just feel so alive, alive, alive

[Drake]Yeah
Yeah Yeah, ugh!
What I tell 'em hoes, "Bow bow bow to me, drop down to ya knees,"
Young Money the Mafia that's where the love cease
I'm in The Dominican, Big Papi Ortiz
doin' target practice all these bitches just aiming to please
shout out to the CEO 500 degrees
shout out to the OVO where we set for T's, awww
N*ggas wanna be friends how coincidental
This supposed to be ya'll year we ain't get the memo
Young King, pay me in gold
40 got a bunch of weed he ain't even roll
These n*ggas be droppin' songs they ain't even cold
Weezy on top and that n*gga ain't even home, yet!
yeah, be very afraid these other rappers getting bodied and carried away
f-ck it me and Nicki Nick gettin' married today
And now you bitches that be hatin can catch a bouquet, ouww
yeah, you a star in my eyes, you and all them white girls party of five
are we drinking a lil more I can hardly decide I can't believe we really made it I'm partly surprised, I swear
d*mn, this one for the books, man!
I swear this shit is as fun as it looks, man!
I'm really tryna make it more than what it is, cuz everybody dies but
not everybody lives!

[Chorus]

I wish that I could have this moment for life, for life, for life
　　Cuz in this moment I just feel so alive, alive, alive

I wish that I could have this moment for life, for life, for life
　　Cuz in this moment I just feel so alive, alive, alive

[Nick Minaj]
This is my moment, I waited all my life I can tell its time
　　drifting away I'm one with the sunsets, I have become alive.

[Chorus]
I wish that I could have this moment for life, for life, for life
　　Cuz in this moment I just feel so alive, alive, alive

I wish that I could have this moment for life, for life, for life
　　Cuz in this moment I just feel so alive, alive, alive.

—Nicki Minaj

Nicki Minaj—Growing Up

If the lyrics of "Moment 4 Life" seem autobiographical, it's because they are. They tell the story of the life of Onika Tanya Maraj, a.k.a. Nicki Minaj, who was born on December 8, 1982 in St. James, a suburb of Trinidad and Tobago's capital city Port of Spain to Carol and Omar, who are of multiracial descent (African, Trinidadian and Indo-Asian). She has two brothers, Makiya and Jelani.

The five-foot-four psychedelic rhythmic powerhouse, who grew up singing in the choir, recounts her childhood "as crazy," saying that her father drank, took drugs and tried to kill her mother by burning down the family home. As a result, when she was three, she says that she and her older brother lived with her grandmother while her mother shuttled back-and forth between Trinidad to New York City in search of a new home.

"A lot of times, when you're from the islands, your parents leave and then send for you because it's easier when they have established themselves; when they have a place to stay, when they have a job. I thought it was gonna be for a few days, it turned into two years without my mother".

At the age of 5, the family, including Omar, moved to the storied New York City. Nicki says that she thought the nightmare was ending, but it was only just beginning as the family settled in South Jamaica, Queens.

"I thought it was gonna be like a castle, like white picket fence, like a fairy tale. I got off the plane and it was cold. I remember the smell…I had never seen snow…I remember the house. I remember that the furniture wasn't put down. It was, like, piled up on each other, and I didn't understand why, 'cause I thought it was gonna look like a big castle."

Omar's demons apparently followed him from Trinidad. The girl with the candy-coated dreams said that her father fell victim to crack cocaine once in the big city. Her hit single, *Moment 4 Life*, would chronicle her fractured childhood and her future life as a star.

"I started hearing a lot of arguing, and I didn't know why, I was always very nervous, very afraid. So I knew that wasn't normal. My father would yell and curse a lot…It was right in the crack era. We didn't know, but he fell victim to crack shortly after he moved to America…When you're on crack, you can't keep a job. And when you can't keep a job, you don't have money. And when you don't have money, you steal. And you steal from your family."

The future MC turned to a land of make-believe to escape the dysfunction, using outlandish voices and role-playing that would later become her hallmark of fame. She used to pretend to be a teacher and a nurse so much so that the family thought she was going to be one or the other. She also saw herself as a guardian of her mother, who worked as a nurse's aide.

"When there was an argument and her father picked up something, she would come and stand in front of me and do like this," her mother said, spreading her arms like wings. "She was so young and just trying to protect me."

As young Nicki Minaj moved through P.S. 45 and on to Elizabeth Blackwell Middle School 210 in Queens, she used drama as salve to her conscience to help navigate her difficult home life.

"To get away from all their fighting, I would imagine being a new person, Cookie' was my first identity—that stayed with me for a while. I went on to Harajuku Barbie, then Nicki Minaj. Fantasy was my reality. I must have been such a fucking annoying little girl," she adds with a self-mocking eye roll. "Everywhere we went I was up singing or acting, like, 'Hey look at me!'"

By the time she was ready for high school, she had theatrical skills enough to audition at Fiorello H. LaGuardia High School, a.k.a. the Fame High School. Initially, she was supposed to sing, but she lost her voice. She was ready to call it quits, but her mother insisted that she try out for the drama program.

"I auditioned for singing, but I didn't get in because I hurt my voice, I was like, *Oh, my God. Get me out of here.*"

"She was so sad," Maraj told E!. "She said, 'Mommy, I want to go home.' I said, 'No, no, there is one more thing. There is the drama. You have to try out for that.'"

"I was used to getting my way, but that was the one thing I remember my mother putting her foot down, I stomped my feet all the way down to the basement where the drama department resides. Within the first 20 minutes I knew that was where I wanted to be. I didn't feel uncomfortable. I didn't feel weird and I got in as a drama major. Thank God she made me stay."

Nicki quickly built a reputation at LaGuardia as a gregarious jokester. She recalled role playing and spitting rhymes in the hall and the classroom.

"To be in a room with a hundred kids and all doing a British accent and they've never been to the U.K., I was like how do you know how to do that? I thought I was the only one."

She recalled on E! that there were only three black students in her class and that most of the white students thought she was crazy.

"All the white people thought I was crazy, I called Ashley Bashley. Andrew I would call him Bandrew. That made me feel better. It quenched some mental thirst and they loved it."

But after graduating from high school, she quickly lost interest in acting when the gigs did not pan out. One of her last acting roles was in 2001 in the off-off Broadway play, *In Case you Forget*, which she won while working as a waitress at Red Lobster.

"It just didn't pan out, I lost the passion for it. I wanted everything really quickly. I went on two auditions. I was like, 'what? I didn't get that role? Oh, forget this.' " I'm done. They don't realize who I am?"

But after finding herself in a 9-to-5 grind, working office jobs and as a waitress, she decided to give music a shot. Getting fired was a wake up call. Her mother recalled being concerned about the decision, but there was not much she could do to stop her.

"I had never given anything my all, I was like, 'you know what, 'I don't care if I end up in a shelter, I'm not going back to work."

II

Lil Wayne Signs Nicki Minaj

"I am honored to have Nicki Minaj as Young Money's First Lady. She is a star."

—*Lil Wayne*

Nicki recalled writing her first rap at the age of 12 when she was in middle school. It happened after she heard her older next-door neighbor spitting rhyme.

"I was like, how did you learn how to do that? I went home and wrote *Cookie's the Name and Chocolate Chip is the Flavor,* the infamous rap, and I waited until she got home, knocked on her door and I spit the rap to her," Nicki recalled. "She called the neighborhood guys and she was like, 'yo, come and listen to her rap. I was thinking she liked the rap, but she was trying to play me, trying to say the rap was so wack. But I was so young. I didn't know. They kept making me say it over and over. They definitely gave me the energy to continue spitting that rap, but they were clearly laughing behind my back."

In the end, the joke was on the neighbor. Nicki, of course, later went on to become a global star.

But her rise to fame was not easy. She made three mixtapes between 2007 and 2009, including *Playtime Is Over* with Dirty Money Records, *Suka Free* on Be and *Beam Me Up Scotty* on Trapaholics Records. She also garnered attention via her MySpace page.

"It was there that Dirty Money Entertainment CEO Fendi first heard her ability to freestyle and first laid eyes on her steamy set of promo shots," according to her Bing Music biography. "…Minaj was a perfect fit for Fendi's urban DVD magazine, *The Come Up*."

It was he who suggested that she change her last name from Maraj to Minaj, according to E!.

She appeared in numerous volumes of *The Come Up*, including number 11, which featured Young Money label boss and rapper Lil Wayne.

"I was like this female right here is amazing," Lil Wayne told E! "She'd be amazing for my label as well. That's when I knew I wanted to sign her… I was like get me in contact with that girl named Nicki."

"He was smitten with me, I guess you could say that. His people reached out to my people. They happened to know each other. The next thing you know I was flying out to meet him and he was telling me about something called Young Money. I was like, *who*?"

They began to build her career through mixtapes like Lil Wayne's *Dedication 3* and Nicki's own *Sucka Free*. Meanwhile, appearances on various remixes—everything from T.I.'s *No Matter What* to Jeffree Star's club track *Cupcakes Taste Like Violence*—helped spread the word.

The 2009 news release announcing the signing of Nicki Minaj said the battle to sign her resulted in a very unique deal with Young Money/Universal, where she retains and owns all of her 360 rights, including merchandising, sponsorships, endorsements, touring and publishing.

"I am honored to have Nicki Minaj as Young Money's First Lady," Lil Wayne said in the new release. "She is a star."

Needless to say, Nicki was also honored.

"To say I'm excited would be an understatement," she said in the release. "It's validation. It's proof. It's empowerment. I represent every little girl in a hood near you. To everyone that supported me two years ago when I was on underground mix-tapes and DVDs and to the people that only caught on two weeks ago, I say thank you. Be proud of yourself. You've given girls all around the world the permission to change the face of female rap."

Nicki and Friends

Nicki Minaj & Lil' Wayne

Nicki Minaj & Rihanna

Nicki Minaj & Rihanna

Nicki Minaj & Jay Leno

Nicki Minaj & Usher

Nicki Minaj & Lauren London

Nicki Minaj & Drake

Nicki Minaj & Lil' Kim

Nicki Minaj & Chris Brown

Nicki Minaj with Katie Perry, Rihanna & Ke$ha

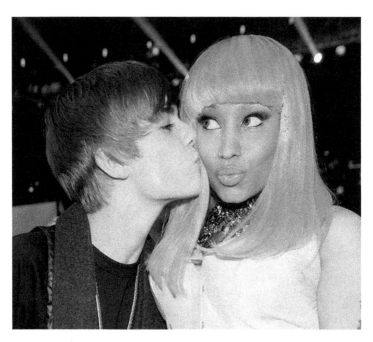

Nicki Minaj & Justin Bieber

Nicki Minaj & Diddy

"I'm the Best"

It was back in '07, did a couple of tapes Did a couple DVD's, made a couple mistakes Didn't know what I was doin', but I put on a cape Now it's which world tour should I go on and take

See you told me I would lose but I won I might cop a million Jimmy Choo's just for fun 'Cause bitches couldn't take what was in me Australia, Sydney, might run up in Disney Out in LA with Lindsey

Got the eye of the tiger, the lion of Judah Now it's me in my time, it's just me in my prime Everything I'm tried to teach 'em, they gon' see it in time Tell them bitches get a stick, I'm done leadin' the blind

Got two shows tonight, that's Brooklyn and Dallas Then a private party at the Buckingham palace Which means I gotta fly like a movie no commercial That's Young Money, Cash Money, ya I'm universal

I hear they comin' for me Because the top is lonely What the fuck they gon' say What the fuck they gon' say

I'm the best bitch, doin' it, doin' it I'm the best bitch, doin' it, doin' it I'm the best, best, best, best I'm the best, best, best, best I'm the best

I remember when I couldn't buy my mother a couch Now I'm sittin' at the closin', bought my mother a house You could never understand why I grind like I do Mikiyah and Gulani while I grind like I do

'Cause even when my daddy was on crack, I was cracked
Now the whole album crack, you ain't gotta skip a track I
ain't gotta get a plaque, I ain't gotta get awards I just walk
up out the door, all the girls will applaud

All the girls will come in, as long as they understand that
I'm fightin' for the girls that never thought they could win
'Cause before they could begin you told 'em it was the end.
But I am here to reverse the curse that they live in

Got two bones to pick, I'ma only choose one You might
get addressed on the second album Which means you can
breath, tell that motherfucker say so To all my bad bitches,
I can see your halo

I hear they comin' for me Because the top is lonely What the
fuck they gon' say What the fuck they gon' say

I'm the best bitch, doin' it, doin' it I'm the best bitch, doin'
it, doin' it I'm the best, best, best, best I'm the best, best,
best, best I'm the best

It's okay, it's okay, long as you know Long as you know Long
as you motherfuckers know I'm the best, best, best, best

I hear they comin' for me Because the top is lonely What the
fuck they gon' say What the fuck they gon' say

I'm the best bitch, doin' it, doin' it I'm the best bitch, doin'
it, doin' it I'm the best...

—Nicki Minaj

21

III

Behind the Making of the First Album—"Pink Friday"

Minaj's rhymes continued to tell her story. The autobiographical, *I'm the Best*, was a hot single on her first album, "Pink Friday", which was released on November 19, 2010. Another single, *Massive Attack*, was released as a test and it bombed.

"*Massive Attack*, the Sean Garrett-produced track that left a lot of people scratching their heads, it seems as though she is still figuring that out. It's the kind of song that makes you feel old—like you're missing something that the kids on designer drugs might understand," Vibe wrote in 2010. "Or maybe it's just not a very good song. Either way, the response has been lukewarm at best."

In response, a defensive Garrett told Vibe, *Massive Attack* was the record she wanted to go with. I think it's a different sound. She wanted to make a statement. She definitely has a different direction for her album and her career than where most people think she wants to go."

Nicki told Vibe that the single was important because it was unexpected.

"It was important for me to do something not everyone thought I was gonna do … People close to me have their preferences, their favorite Nicki thing, and I have to stand up sometimes and block out the noise."

But her first single, *Your Love*, reached No. 14 on Billboard's Hot 100s and the Top 10 of Hot R&B/Hop-Hop songs. Young Money Barbie became the first female rapper to be included on MTV's Annual Hottest MC List and first female rapper to hit the chart unaccompanied since Missy Elliott in 2002.

"In the summer of 2010, Nicki was the acid-tongued "two" to Drake's "one" in Lil Wayne's Young Money one-two punch," MTV reports. "With her debut album still on the way, she was murdering features left and right…'When she hit the scene, she was just like the pretty girl alongside Wayne,' said Rahman Dukes, MTV News' director of hip-hop news. 'Drake was really the next one that everyone was looking out for.' "

Her fame grew after she appeared on Saturday Night Live as a musical guest in January 2011 and performed singles, *Right Thru Me* and *Moment 4 Life*. A month later, the album soared to No. 1 on the Billboard 200. In May, 2011, her popular hit single, *Super Bass*, was released and sailed to No. 8 and was certified quadruple-platinum by the Recording Industry Association of America (RIAA).

Nicki's song *"Super Bass"* was just a bonus track on the album, but it won over fans including squeaky-clean Taylor Swift and Selena Gomez, both of whom jumped on the record, rapping along line for line to the infectious track, *Bass* may have even helped Nicki score a spot opening for Britney Spears on her Femme Fatale Tour.

Her role-playing and alter-egos took center stage with the release of *Pink Friday*, where she introduced Roman Zolanski on *Roman's Revenge*. During a stop at Wendy William's show, she hinted at the target of the song.

"On "Roman's Revenge," featuring a rowdy verse from Eminem as Slim Shady, Nicki embodies her Brit character, Roman Zolanski. Word that bitch mad 'cause I took the spot/ Well, bitch, if you ain't sh—-ing, then get off the pot/ Got some n—-az out in Brooklyn that'll off your top.' "

Many hip-hop fans assumed Nicki was talking about Lil Kim, including the Queen Bee herself.

"I don't get into that, … I feel like my music, my fans know everything that's going on. Every time I talk, every time I spit raps, my fans know who I'm talking about, what I'm talking about. I don't have to sit up here and detail it. No. For what?"

She has said that Zolanski was a demon inside her and her "twin brother". She has also described him as gay. Following her win for best hip-hop video on MTV Video Music Awards, she told reporters to expect more of her male alter ego on her second album, *Pink Friday: Roman Reloaded*.

"The new album is going to have a lot of Roman on it," she said, according to The Hollywood Reporter. "And if you're not familiar with Roman, then you will be familiar with him very soon. He's the boy that lives inside of me. He's a lunatic and he's gay and he'll be on there a lot."

She added, according to The Hollywood Reporter: "I have a lot of surprises that I don't want to give away," she said. "Just know that everybody will be more than satisfied with the new album."

Indeed, *Pink Friday*, sealed Minaj's fate as a rising star. Within a month of its release, it earned Platinum certification in the United States.

"Nicki Minaj will not be contained," Marc Hogan wrote in a review of the album in Spin . "Not to 16-bar verses. Not to one persona. Not even to hip-hop. Brought up in Jamaica, Queens, and taught to be a star at New York City's "Fame" school (LaGuardia High School of Music & Art and Performing Arts), the MC born Onika Maraj has more alter egos than most pop stars have nicknames. With three promising mixtapes and a streak of spotlight-hogging guest verses, she's established herself as the best (avowedly bisexual) female in hip-hop's "no homo" boys' club. But anyone who comes to her official full-length, Pink Friday, expecting more of the raw, terrifically unhinged rhyming that stole Kanye West's "Monster" will be disappointed. Rap's most hotly anticipated debut works best if you don't think of it as a rap album at all."

But releasing a totally un-rap album was no accident, Hogan opined. Like her Young Money label mates, Lil Wayne and Drake, "albeit with less Auto-Tune and a lot less innuendo, Minaj turns toward frothy, hooky pop on her new album. That means you'll hear her singing, which is nothing exceptional, as well as rapping, which is still spectacular: cartoonish, clever, and endlessly flexible."

With the release of *Pink Friday,* Nicki Minaj was simply "BLAZIN"

"BLAZIN"

I fly, I fly high, I'm blazing, I'm blazing, feels like I'm blazing I fly, I fly high, I'm blazing, I'm blazing, feels like I'm blazing Feels like I'm blazing

How could it be, little me had the power to be The best B in the league inevitably But could it be little me, you was heckling me Now it's monotony when I regularly

I catch wreck on recreation So I exceed all your expectations Because I got it in 'em, I kill 'em and then I skin 'em The contract is on but I am the addendum

So where my dawgs at, Randy Matter fact, get off my dick bitch, Andy 'Cause everything is fine and dandy Go against me now, I dare you, Bambi

Half a million dollars just to upgrade the car show I ain't even detonate the bombs and the arsenal Before the storm comes the calm Hope you can take the heat like LeBron

I'm the best now Anybody with some money should invest now Soccer mom needs to organize a pep rall' You game over bitch, Gatorade, wet towel

Muthafuckers ain't ready, they neva' been As long as I am in the game, you'll never win I'm on that different type of high, heroin Put on my cape and hit the sky, heroine

I fly, I fly high, I'm blazing, I'm blazing, feels like I'm blazing I fly, I fly high, I'm blazing, I'm blazing, feels like I'm blazing I fly, I fly high, I'm blazing, I'm blazing, feels like I'm blazing I fly, I fly high, I'm blazing, I'm blazing, feels like I'm blazing

This is the moment, grab your Kodak while I'm flying With a flow that is the greatest throwback since that Nolan Ryan And the days been crazy and the nights even wilder And the lights even brighter, baby stand next to my fire

Only higher is Messiah or notes from Mariah 'Rari six hundred horses, that's my chariot of fire Where we flying, they can't find us, all them broke days behind us I just took your whole life and redesigned it

I think I'm Marc Jacobs, I think I'm Lagerfeld I think without makeup, you still bad as hell I'ma grab your waist, then I'ma grab your face and Then I'ma taste it, then I'ma blaze it

—Nicki Minaj

IV

Nicki's Launch Toward Superstardom

Just like her hit single states, Nicki Minaj's career was Blazin.' She successfully integrated what she learned while studying drama at LaGuardia with her music, captivating millions and boasting a loyal and global fan base from New York to London to Japan.

The starlet, also known as Harajuki Barbie, calls her fans Barbz, Barbs, or Barbies has about 13.6 million Twitter followers. The name is a hat tip to her early release tape, *Barbie World.* She is quite active on Twitter and corresponds regularly with her fans, letting them know when she is in what town and country for a tour.

During a post in July, 2012, she told fans at 11 p.m., "Barbz, if u MUST know, we're editing the rest of PTA! That's why I'm still up." PTA, of course being *Pound the Alarm,* a single from second album, *Pink Friday: Roman Reloaded.*

But like with most social media, she has had a love-hate relationship with Twitter. In April, she made a dramatic departure from Twitter after "Roman Reloaded" was leaked early. She left 13 million followers in a lurch.

"Like seriously, it's but so much a person can take. Good f*cking bye," she wrote before signing off".

"It looked like the pop star was only going to reprimand the site in question—called NickiDaily.com, which now appears to be shut down—for illegally distributing the songs from Nicki's *Pink Friday: Roman Reloaded* album, when she blocked it from her Twitter account," OMG reported. "But eventually she decided to leave all of her followers out in the cold. Talk about one bad apple spoiling the bunch!"

While filming her appearance on BBC's Graham Norton Show, E reported that Nicki said a voice told her to do it.

"A voice in my head told me to delete my Twitter and that's what I did," she explained, according to E. "I had 13 million followers and I hope they will wait for me. I reply all the time and get to know them by name and I have a really personal bond with them…not all 13 million, but at least 10 of them a day."

Fans pleaded with her to change her mind.

"Nope. Nope Stop playing @NICKIMINAJ WE NEED YOU," a follower tweeted, according to OMG. "We learned our lesson. we took lots of things for granted. NOT NO MORE. PLEASE COME BACK!"

"That depressing moment when you go to @NICKIMINAJ account and it says this user does not exist :(another fan lamented.

While it appeared that she had lost followers, she gained them back and more when she returned to Twitter.

She also made the rounds on television talk shows as she won the hearts of the even the tiniest of fans, making a splash on "The Ellen DeGeneres Show" to surprise two *Super Bass* fans, 8-year-old Sophia Grace and her 5-year-old cousin Rosie. The two made a YouTube video that went viral and were on the show to do a redux. Upon seeing Nicki, little Sophia squealed with delight and jumped into her arms.

Fans weren't the only ones taking note of Nicki's skills.

Known as a top MC from her mix tape days, she also became a highly sought after vocalist. She served as a key vocalist on Trey Songz's *Bottoms Up*, Usher's *Lil Freak* and Kanye West's wildly popular *Monster*. In 2011, she was featured on David Guetta's album, *Nothing But the Beat*. She and Rihanna collaborated on their "Fly" music video, which debuted at pre-show for the 2011 MTV Video Music Awards.

"Nicki's been a magnetic, polarizing, scene-stealing figure for something like a year, but her masterfully manic verse here feels like the moment where she becomes a full-on *star*, an undeniable force in rap," Tom Breihan wrote in 2010 in a Pitchfork review of *Monster*. "She's a whirlwind of energy, showing her full repertoire of nutso voices and kicking the living fuck out of the beat, sounding like she's having an absolute blast the whole time: 'Yeah, I'm in that Tonka, color of Willy Wonka! You could be the king but watch the queen conquer!' "

Madonna, forever trying to stay relevant, even enlisted the MC's support on her single, *Give Me All Your Love*, from the album, *MDNA*, which was released in 2012. Madonna also used Nicki's popularity to generate much needed buzz before the album's release with a kiss. Cyberspace was intoxicated by news that the two had kissed. Nicki herself helped fan the flames among the Barbz with a simple tweet: "OH MY Finggg Gahhhhh!!!!! MADONNA jus kissed me!!!!! On the lips!!!!!!! It felt Sooooo good. Soooo soft!!!! *passes out* aaahhhhh!!!!!!!!!!" Later, she lit up the erstwhile sex icon's halftime Super Bowl XLVI show with a flamboyant appearance as a sideline cheerleader decked in a blonde wig and colorful outfit.

Alas, the little girl from Queens who was laughed at when she first spit rhymes to a neighbor, wrote this in her rising stardom in her hit song *Blazin.'*

> *"This is the moment, grab your Kodak while I'm flying with a flow that is the greatest throwback since that Nolan Ryan,"* she rhymes. *"And the days been crazy and the nights even wilder and the lights even brighter, baby stand next to my fire. Flying, they can't find us, all them broke days behind us I just took your whole life and redesigned it."*

"Fly"

I came to win, to fight, to conquer, to thrive I came to win, to survive, to prosper, to rise to fly, to fly

I wish today it will rain all day Maybe that will kinda make the pain go away *Trying to forgive you for abandoning me* Praying but I think I'm still an angel away

Angel away, yeah strange in a way *Maybe that is why I chase strangers away They got their guns out aiming at me But I become near when they aiming at me*

Me, me, me against them *Me against enemies, me against friends Somehow they both seem to become one A sea full of sharks and they all smell blood*

They start coming and I start rising Must be surprising, I'm just surmising I win, thrive, soar, higher, higher, higher More fire

I came to win, to fight, to conquer, to thrive I came to win, to survive, to prosper, to rise To fly, to fly

Everybody wanna try to box me in Suffocating every time it locks me in Paint they own pictures, then they crop me in But I will remain where the top begins

'Cause I am not a word, I am not a line I am not a girl that can ever be defined I am not fly, I am levitation I represent an entire generation

I hear the criticism loud and clear That is how I know that the time is near See we become alive in a time of fear And I ain't got no motherfucking time to spare

Cry my eyes out for days upon days Such a heavy burden placed upon me But when you go hard your nay's become yea's Yankee Stadium with Jay's and Kanye's

I came to win, to fight, to conquer, to thrive I came to win, to survive, to prosper, to rise To fly, to fly

Get ready for it, get ready for it, get ready for it I came to win Get ready for it, get ready for it, get ready for it

I came to win, to fight, to conquer, to thrive I came to win, to survive, to prosper, to rise To fly, to fly

—Nicki Minaj

V

Nicki Minaj: Fashion Icon

Since her high school and mixtape days, Nicki Minaj's singular fashion sense and sensibility has turned heads. She has projected her style through her numerous and defiant alteregos, including Roman and his mother Martha Zolanski, Harajuku Barbie, Nicki the Boss, Rosa; Nicki the Ninja…all of whom parade through the pastel schizopolis of her bizarro music-video universe; David Wallace-Wells wrote in New York Magazine. "And all of whom are dressed to the nines, in an à la carte assemblage of Cyndi Lauper gone cyberpunk, sexed-up Missy Elliott, black-light anime, Japanese street fashion, and hip-hop booty mag. Among a laundry pile of other influences from the anything-goes fashion future…

The whole circus is dazzling and code-cracking genius, since pop markets run by the same laws as any other: grow or die. The problem of being sexy in rap has forced all of Nicki's flummoxed emcee predecessors the other way, into little whirlpools of self-caricature. (See, along with Kim and Elliott, MC Lyte, Da Brat, and Foxy Brown.) She shuns comparisons to her contemporary Lady Gaga, although both have transformed a generation with their corybantic performances and colorful outfits. She told ABC's Juju Chang for Nightline in April 2012 that she dislikes being called the "Black Lady Gaga."

"We're in completely different lanes," Nicki told Chang. "I'm a rapper … Gaga's a fantastic artist, you know, she paved her way. She's opened her own lane. But I think that I have my own lane.

And we never cross. Ever. So, you know, I really don't get the comparison anymore. Our music doesn't sound the same. Our stage presence is not the same. I just can't see the similarities."

But both she and Lady Gaga like to turn heads on the red carpet with wild outfits. Nicki raised more than a few brows when she appeared at the iHeartRadio Music Festival in September, 2011 sporting a chicken wing necklace, which appropriately described by MTV, was "paired with an embellished pink tutu dress, hot pink bra, space-age tights, larger-than-life blonde permed hair, and plastic neon accessories."

"The most uh-mazing thing about this particular necklace is that it has totally been Minaj-ified," Chrissy Mahlmeister wrote for MTV, "It's HOT PINK. Like, what screams Barbie more than that? Nothing. Also, paired with a buttload of gold chains makes it absolutely POIFECT for Ms. Minaj. Just when we thought it couldn't get any better than her sporting ice cream and a soft pretzel around her neck, Nicki pulled out ALL the stops with this edible accessory."

Eyes popped in Tokyo when she wore a popcorn dress to greet fans. The ensemble was made of molded bustier with popcorn bulging from the top, matched with a red and white angular skirt.

Who can forget when MTV dissected her outfit.

MTV's Andi Teran dissected it this way:

Nicki Minaj was nothing short of a JOYOUSLY BIZARRE REVELATION at this year's VMAs with her much photographed and blogged about futuristic candy-pop, Harajuku-esque, club kid ensemble. (Did we forget to add cartoon robot baby-nurse? Please FORGIVE.) The Barbie-loving Best Hip Hop video winner (ONE FOR THE LADIES!!!), sent the entire VMA red carpet pre-show crowd into a screaming FRENZY when she arrived, her typically diminutive figure eLONGated by a towering beehive of bubble gum pink and lemonade yellow hair buns resting atop her head like undulating saltwater taffy (YUMMM).

But it wasn't until she stood still, a Whoozit-inspired stuffed toy dangling all the way to the ground from her finger, that we had a gummi bear-induced EUREKA moment. Could Nicki Minaj's outfit be an ode to the candy raver days of yore?

The Outfit:

Just look at this accessory EXPLOSION. There's so much going on here. It's as if a ROBOT ANIME PRINCESS has come to life forcing you to stare, trance-like, into her metallic prism peplum while thinking about nothing but dancing ice cream cones and creepy-happy dolls. Despite the hard edges of Nicki's metal dress overlay, there's a softness to the rest of her outfit from the pouffe-y pink underskirt to the layers of socks and light color scheme. Candy ravers are all about sharing love (and candy), and we wouldn't doubt that ANIME NICKI wants to do the same, but we're afraid to hug her for fear of getting jabbed in the hip.

The Hair:

Nothing says HAPPY FUN TIME (the motto of EVERY candy raver) like delicious piles of pink lemonade doughnut buns. We love that something this voluminous rests on a face-framing, pink-tinged 60s 'do (reminiscent of Aretha Franklin circa 1968). Despite it's unexpected color combo and towering height, we think this Nicki hair looks feminine and really rather pretty.

The Mask

We can't decide if Nicki's Shojono Tomo 'Thander Eye Mask' is more of the is-she-sick or is-she-a-pop-ninja variety, but either way WE LIKE IT. Way to throw an invisible-lips curveball, Miss M! CAPTIVATING!

The Necklace

Oh, HAY, Onch Movement ice cream necklace that wants to crawl into our oversized ballerina jewelry boxes! We canNOT believe that this pink and blue chained plastic NECKPIECE looks so perfect with the rest of this CRAY CRAY BANANAS ensemble. We can't, for the fuzzy backpacked life of us, figure out HOW and WHY this works but it does. It is, indeed, a frozen DELIGHT.

The Dress:

Excuse us, but is this hand stitched METAL? Nicki's Amato Couture dress is an unusual balance of hard and soft. The pointy edges of the outer dress seem to work with the lace-y underpinnings, and—WAIT—is it just us or are her purple bloomers trying to say something? Like, an actual MESSAGE?

The Doll:

Yet another piece from Japanese artist Shojono Tomo, we think this cat-eared giraffe doll just wants to play, you know? Any self-respecting plush doll baby with dancing pink bears on her tummy does, right?

The Socks:

Shojono Tomo really knocked it out with the number of items she contributed to Nicki Minaj's VMA MASTERPIECE (yeah, we decreed it), and these layered socks and legwarmers are also from what we imagine is her giggling magical elf-factory workshop. Just look at these layers of pink lips, Bambi parts, and totally random RED FURRY CREATURE TOES! If these don't make you HAPPY GO LUCKY PARTY FUN TIME, we don't know what will.

Minaj fever has indeed been born. She has also become a marketing bonanza. In February 2012, she became the face of MAC's Viva Glam campaign. The company introduced her "scene-stealing pink lipstick," whose sales proceeds are donated to the provide support to those living with AIDS.

Mattel created a one-of-a-kind Nicki Minaj Barbie for auction at CharityBuzz.com, Billboard reported. Bidding started at $1,000 for the doll, which was dressed in boots.

"The Barbie itself is a pink explosion, with mini-Minaj decked out in towering boots, signature long hair and an outfit made of sparkly toule and diamonds," Billboard wrote. "

Billboard quoted Stefani Yocky, a Barbie spokesman, saying: "Barbie is obviously a pop culture icon. She's been in the spotlight for over 50 years, and strikes that chord with girls of all ages in terms of being representative of the times. And Nicki is a big part of pop culture and also huge within the fashion industry, as well as a big Barbie fan."

Critics of her style would be wise to heed the words of a rhyme she spits in *Fly*: "'Cause I am not a word, I am not a line I am not a girl that can ever be defined I am not fly, I am levitation I represent an entire generation."

Her most controversial performance and costume were yet to come with the release of her second album.

Nicki Minaj Fashion Icon Rising to the Top

"Roman Holiday"

Take your medication, Roman
Take a short vacation, Roman
You'll be okay
You need to know your station, Roman
Some alterations on your clothes and your brain
Take a little break, little break
From your silencing
There is so much you can take, you can take
I know how bad you need a Roman holiday
Roman holiday
A Roman holiday
You done, you tight?
You suck at life?
You don't want a round three?
You done suffered twice
Worship the queen and you might get passed
Keep it real, these bitches couldn't wipe my ass
Anyway, stylist, go get Bulgari
I am the ultimate Svengali
You bitches can't even spell that
You, you hoes buggin'
Repel that
Let me tell you this sister
I am, I am colder than a blister
Cause my flow's is sick
And I'm a lunatic
And this can't be cured with no elixir
Cuz y'all know who the fuck, what the fuck I do
I done put the pressure to every thug
I knew Quack quack to a duck and a chicken too
Put the hyena in a freakin' zoo
Take your medication, Roman
Take a short vacation, Roman

You'll be okay
You need to know your station, Roman
Some alterations on your clothes and your brain
Take a little break, little break
From your silencing
There is so much you can take, you can take
I know how bad you need a Roman holiday
Roman holiday A Roman holiday
Witch, twitch, bitch! Mother fucker's right, this is World
War 6
This right here might make a bitch die
And this right here gonna make a bitch cry
And if I'm being honest I am such a great guy
But this what I do when a bitch breaks off
I'mma put her in a dungeon under, under
No those bitches ain't eating they dying of hunger
Mother fucker I need
Who the fuck is this hoe
And yes maybe just a touch of tourettes
Get my wigs Terrence go and get my berets
Take your medication, Roman

Take a short vacation, Roman
…A Roman holiday
Come all ye faithful Joyful and triumphant
I am Roman Zolanski

—Nicki Minaj

VI

The 54th Grammy Awards Ceremony

The 54th Grammy Awards Ceremony at the Staples Center in Los Angeles on February 12, 2012 was Nicki Minaj's coming out party of sorts. Already a monster in the music industry and among the Barbz, she made an impression upon the world with her performance of *Roman Holiday* and *Roman's Revenge*, which included dancing priests, an exorcism and levitation. She also introduced her wild alter ego Roman Zolanski. His mother, Martha, was there, too. Lady Gaga's former choreographer Laurieann Gibson orchestrated the act.

"Nicki Minaj was so much fun for me, and it was like a real breath of fresh air, and musically, to get back to the rap game, to see a female MC dominate the pop charts, this, historically, for me, I feel a bit of responsibility," Gibson told MTV News about working with Nicki. "When I did 'The Rain,' that video for Missy [Elliott], and just with Puff and the evolution of Bad Boy Records and my responsibility there and the pressure to maintain dominant rappers [on major award shows] and not let them lose street credibility, the years of all that torture … and all of those moments. When I got back to Nicki, I was so happy to be in that soulful music again, in that fight, in the idea that rap is not dead and that somebody like her can be many things in many genres and not be limited."

"I love [when] I heard Roman Reloaded. I loved her delivery. I love the way she flows," Gibson added. "So the Pink Friday Tour is really good and it's kind of like a glimpse back to what a real rap show is. It's intimate but big at the same time."

Not everyone was impressed or amused. She received scathing reviews and many were befuddled and offended by the act, including the Catholic League.

"Perhaps the most vulgar was the sexual statement that showed a scantily clad female dancer stretching backwards while an altar boy knelt between her legs in prayer," said Bill Donohue, the president of the Catholic League, CBS New York reported.

But Nicki did not back down, explaining to the Associated Press that she performed a preview of a play. She told the AP that her performance, which featured a film clip, was partly inspired by the 1973 movie "The Exorcist." Some speculated that they should have known she was up to something when she showed up on the red carpet decked in an oversized red robe on the arm of an older man who was dressed as a pope.

"I don't know what is the big issue? You know how people write plays and movies? That's what I did. I wrote that and I gave the world a tiny little preview of what was to come. And so I have to perform it on the set in which it would be in the movie, right?"

If the name Nicki Minaj didn't register with anyone before the 54th Grammy Awards, it certainly did afterwards.

"I definitely felt like she was reaching out to the mainstream with this performance, trying to make that full leap into the pop world," AllHipHop.com founder Chuck Creekmur told MTV News of Nicki's controversial act. "She'll definitely have people talking. Obviously, we've seen this before with Madonna and Lady Gaga—especially Gaga."

Ken Ehrlich, the executive producer of the Grammys, told CBS' This Morning after the Grammys that it was important to allow artists to be creative.

"Look, one of the things that is always very important to us, we don't like to restrict an artist's creative freedom," he told CBS'. "She came to us with that idea. Often the ideas are ours, sometimes they're the acts we work with."

Ehrlich scoffed when CBS asked if he thought Nicki delivered a strong performance.

"At that one? I didn't say great," he told CBS. "I looked at that one and said, OK, I knew about her alter ego, I'm kind of aware of what that was, and I definitely had some questions about it."

Indeed, while Grammy viewers were not familiar with Roman, Nicki's British alter ego, he was well known among her devoted Barbz. He also made an appearance with Eminem's alter ego, Slim Shady, on *Roman's Revenge*. Born of Nicki's own rage and disappointment, the alter ego also has a mother, Martha, who appears on the *Moment 4 Life* video.

"Everybody knows my favorite alter ego is Roman, He's bad. That's why I like Roman. I think I started liking Roman more because everybody else starting like Roman, so he became my favorite. People are expecting him to do some real craziness on the next album."

In an effort to generate more buzz for her sophomore release, Nicki made it clear that she wanted the character to be the star. "And if you're not familiar with Roman, then you will be familiar with him very soon, he's the boy that lives inside of me. He's a lunatic and he's gay, and he'll be on there a lot."

If Nicki wanted to generate buzz about her sophomore release and extend the reach of her popularity beyond her Barbz, her mission was accomplished. The wildly colorful Nicki Minaj and her eclectic ensemble of alter egos had roared their way to the tip of everyone's tongue.

"Roman Reloaded"

I guess I went commercial, just shot a commercial
When I flew to the set though, I ain't fly commercial
And your ad is global, yup ad is global
When we shot it was a lot of different agricultures
So I laugh at hopefuls Nicki pop, only thing that's pop is
my endorsement op
Fuck around I had to go and reinforce the block
Bang, my shit bang, b-bang bang

Bang, my shit bang, b-bang bang
Yo, Is it me or did I put these rap bitches on the map
again
You mad 'cause I'm at the Grammys in the Vatican
You in the booth, but I'm who you be channelin'
Why they never bring your name up at the panel then
Hottest MC's, top five
You need money, I got mine More knots than Eric from
Basketball Wives (Ya digggg?)
Bang, my shit bang, b-bang bang

Bang, my shit bang, b-bang bang
I couldn't do your TV show I needed 10 more mil Not 10
on the back, I need 10 on signin'
Give that shit to a washed up bitch, I'm winnin' If I had
a label I would never sign you hoes
Take bitches to school then I Colombine these hoes I
hear the slick shit, bitch you watch All you hoes cryin',
Christopher Bosh
Bang, my shit bang, b-bang bang

Bang, my shit bang, b-bang bang
Ayo now when I tell em' that it's Barbie bitch
Yes I really do mean that it's Barbie Ask Mattel, they
auction my Barbie bitch Raggedy Ann could never be a
Barbie bitch
You at the bottom of the barrel, scrapin' I'm out in LA at
the Ice Age tapin'
I'm chillin' at the top, I got ample time
Bite me, Apple sign Hahaa

—Nicki Minaj

VII

Behind the Making of "Pink of Friday: Roman Reloaded"

Nicki Minaj racked up her second No. 1 album on the Billboard 200 with the release of "Pink Friday: Roman Reloaded", on April 3, 2012 in the U.S., selling 253,000 copies, according to Nielsen SoundScan. Sales were slightly better than expected after industry sources speculated that sales would land between 215,000 to 235,000. She became the first female rapper to debut at Number 1 on the U.K. Charts with "Pink Friday: Roman Reloaded" and she is the first female hip-hop artist to propel her brand into a worldwide operation. She also hit No. 1 in Japan.

"Roman Reloaded" followed her successful debut release, "Pink Friday," which soared to No. 1 on the February 19, 2011 chart, just as her hit single, "Super Bass" was peaking, reports show. "Pink Friday" launched at No. 2 on the Billboard chart dated December 11, 2010, selling 375,000, Nielsen SoundScan reports. Its sales were sparked, in part, by holiday shopping after its Thanksgiving weekend release. The album also sailed to the top of the U.K. album charts, selling 47,000 copies in the first week, making Nicki Minaj the first female rapper to earn such an accomplishment. The album also peaked at one in Canada and Scotland and within the top five in Australia and New Zealand, reports show.

Also, along the way, she managed to become the first female solo artist to post seven singles on the Billboard top 100 at once. Not bad for a little girl, who had pink and blue cotton candy dreams.

"Doing the Super Bowl with Madonna doesn't really change Nicki Minaj's personal goals," Nicki told Miss Info in a Complex Magazine interview in March 2012, a month before the album's scheduled drop. "My goal right now is still to put out "Pink Friday: Roman Reloaded", sell five million copies eventually, and tour every country in the world. That's what I've been working toward. So while the world is talking about, 'Oh my God, I can't believe Nicki Minaj was at the Super Bowl!' I'm mixing and mastering my music. In my scheme of things it's way bigger.' "

In a great promotion stunt, she shared her excitement about the album with her Barbz in a tweet that went viral on March 2, 2012: "I am ABSOLUTELY in LOVE w/this f@%#ing ALBUM!!!!!!! Like!!! AbsoFCNGlutely in LOVE barbz!!!!!!!!!!!!"

The gamble worked. "Roman Reloaded" further established Nicki as a force in the music industry. Her sophomore release blew pop legend Madonna's MDNA from the No. 1 slot, forcing it to drop to No. 8, down 86.7 percent. It was a rough fall for Madonna, the former reigning queen of pop, whose MDNA debuted at No. 1, with 359,000 in sales. It was the largest drop in the largest second-week percentage decline for a No. 1-debuting album since Nielsen SoundScan began tracking sales in 1991, Billboard reports. The record was previously held by Lady Gaga's "Born This Way," which fell 84.27 percent during its second week on the chart dated June 18, 2011. "Born This Way" launched at No. 1 with 1.11 million sales, and then sold only 174,000 in its second week at the top of the chart, Billboard reports.

Released through Universal Republic Records (Universal Music Group), Young Money Entertainment, the album was produced by the superstars, including: Ester Dean, Rico Beats, Hitboy, RedOne, Oak and Flip. Beside Lil Wayne, she worked with a screed of artists, including Drake, Chris Brown, 2 Chainz, Rick Ross, Nas, Young Jeezy, Beenie Man, Bobby V and Cam'ron. It is comprised of two parts. The first part is comprised mostly of hip hop, while the second half is comprised of pop and dance music.

"There's more surprises this time," Andrew "Pop" Wansel, a producer who worked on Your Love, told Rap-Up. "I think she's proven, like, 'Yo, I can rap. I'm probably the best girl to really do this shit ever.' Now she's more comfortable and she's having a little more fun."

Singles from the album soared to the top of the charts. On Billboard's Bubbling Under Hot 100s, "Marilyn Monroe" reached No. 4; "Roman Holiday" hit No. 13 and "Whip It" reached 23. On the UK Singles Chart, "Pound the Alarm" entered at No. 79 and at No. 40 on the Canadian Hot 100.

First announced via Twitter in November 2011, the album was initially slated to be released on February 12, 2012 and "Va Va Voom" was scheduled to be the first single for Rhythmic and Top40/Mainstream radio. But plans changed after the album was beset by delays. A new release date was set in April and "Starships" became the lead single. On the same day that it was released to iTunes on February 14, 2012, the single premiered during On Air with Ryan Seacrest. It glided to No. 9 on Billboard Hot 100, giving her a second solo hit, following "Super Bass".

"Starships" skyrocketed to the top of the charts across the globe, peaking at No. 5 on the Billboard Hot 100. It became her second Top 10 arrival, following her runaway 2011 hit, "Super Bass". "Stupid Hoe" and "Roman Reloaded" were promotional singles. A third promotional single, "Roman in Moscow", did not make the album.

The second single from the album, "Right by My Side", featuring Chris Brown, rose to No. 51 on Billboard Hot 100 and to No. 21 on U.S. Hot R&B/Hip-Hop Songs. It also rose to No. 70 as well as peaking at number 70 in the UK. "Beez in the Trap", with 2 Chainz, was released in April 2012 as the first urban single and peaked at No. 48 on the Billboard Hot 100 and at No. 8 on the rap charts, reports show.

Joshua Berkman, a Cash Money A & R and producer, discussed making the album and working with Nicki with HitQuarters.

"With Nicki specifically, it's all about the particular sound she wants and not everybody can make that sound," Berkman told HitQuarters. "She's very particular about her beats and wouldn't just rap or sing on anything—I could give her a thousand tracks and she may only like one or two."

Berkman credits Lil Wayne with Nicki's development as an artist.

"With Nicki you have to give all the credit to Wayne," Berkman told HitQuarters. "Wayne was the one that was in with all the Young Money artists every single night, teaching them. That's how the whole Young Money album ['We Are Young Money'] came about. He's the genius behind that. But most of all you have to give it to her for being such an incredible artist and hard worker."

When Vibe senior editor Clover Hope asked Nicki to describe the album in layman's terms just before its release, she declined, saying she couldn't be boxed in.

"It's going in a very free, exhilarating direction in terms of me owning who I am and me enjoying the process of making music," Nicki said. "I think that when you get the album you'll feel as if I had absolutely no boundaries. That's probably the best way to explain it so that you understand. The album just has no boundaries. The album cannot be boxed in."

When Hope pushed, Nicki explained: "You know what, I cannot break my album down into how the normal person like yourself would break an album down and say, well this is rap and this is pop.

There is no rap or pop for me. It's Nicki Minaj. It's one collective body of amazing work. You'll feel it. I don't like the labels because sometimes just by one word or one label, a person can take that the wrong way and apply a negative spin to that. So I don't give my music labels."

Reviews of the album ran the gamut. But it was clear that Nicki's popularity was exploding.

Jody Rosen of Rolling Stone wrote:

> Nicki Minaj is a purist's nightmare. She doesn't just straddle pop categories; she dumps them in a Cuisinart, whips them to a frothy purée, and then trains a guided missile at the whole mess. She is a rapper's rapper, a master of flow and punch lines, with skills to please the most exacting gatekeepers of hip-hop street cred. But she's a bubblegum starlet as well, delivering confections to the nation's mall rats. "I'm in the HOV lane," Nicki boasts on her second LP. It's true: She's one of the few performers who can rival Jay-Z's blend of artistic bona fides and sheer star power.
>
> But Nicki is also in the Gaga lane, the Bowie lane, the Missy Elliott and Gary Glitter and Katy Perry and Betty Boop lanes. (By the sound of "Right by My Side"—a blustery duet with Chris Brown—she can cruise in the Jordin Sparks lane, too.) Then there's the Roman Zolanski lane. "Roman Reloaded" opens with Minaj—a biracial woman from Queens via Trinidad—ranting in the voice of her (Polish?) homosexual "twin brother" alter ego. In the same song, she takes on the voice of Martha Zolanski, Roman's mother, singing in a cartoon Cockney accent. "Take your medication, Roman," counsels Minaj/Martha. "Quack, quack to a duck and a chicken, too/Put the hyena in a freakin' zoo," answers Minaj/ Roman. Later, she bursts into "O Come, All Ye Faithful."

She's just limbering up. On *Roman Reloaded*, the energy never flags—it's the rare filler-free mega-pop album, an achievement for a record that stretches to 19 songs and 69 minutes. Minaj fans dismayed by her post-"Super Bass" turn toward pop will be cheered up by the red-meat hip-hop here. There's booming triumphalism ("Champion"), electro-rap boastfests ("Beez in the Trap") and a couple of collaborations with her mentor Lil Wayne in which she more than justifies the claim that ends the album: *I am the female Weezy.*"

—Jody Rosen, Rolling Stone

In a Gawker review, Rich Juzwiak ripped into the album, calling it a mess, cheap sounding with lazy hooks.

"It contained little sense of what Nicki Minaj was other than a pop star who sometimes rapped and sometimes did so cleverly," Juzwiak wrote. "*Roman Reloaded* is the Wicked Witch of the West to its predecessor's East. It's worse than the other one was.

The stakes feel higher here because *Pink Friday* helped turn Nicki Minaj into a standalone superstar. Now is the time to assert herself—and yet this album finds Nicki more fractured than ever. From the start, she's flaunted her duality, turning decades of the multitasking burden put on women in hip-hop into a marketing tool that allows her to be potentially all things to all people. (It's a grand tradition she's capitalizing on."

Nicki brushed back critics, especially to critics who ask if she's straying from her mixtape and hip hop roots with pop-like songs like "Starships". Did she need to get back to her roots?

"You ain't gotta take Nicki Minaj back to nothin, Nicki Minaj knows who I am."

She very well could add a line from *Roman Reloaded* to that response: "*Yo, Is it me or did I put these rap bitches on the map again.*

You mad 'cause I'm at the Grammys in the Vatican. You in the booth, but I'm who you be channelin.'"

While everybody was busy being a critic, Nicki convened her alter ego to prepare them for a world tour for the Barbz.

"Starships"

Let's go to the beach, each
Let's go get away
They say, what they gonna say?
Have a drink, clink, found the bud light
Bad bitches like me, is hard to come by
The patron own, let's go get it on
The zone own, yes, I'm in the zone
Is it two, three? Leave a good tip
I'ma blow off my money and don't give two shits

I'm on the floor, floor
I love to dance
So give me more, more, 'till I can't stand
Get on the floor, floor
Like it's your last chance
If you want more, more
Then here I am
Starships were meant to fly
Hands up, and touch the sky
Can't stop, 'cause we're so high
Let's do this one more time
Starships were meant to fly
Hands up, and touch the sky
Let's do this one last time

—Nicki Minaj

VIII

Nicki Minaj on Tour

Pink Friday: Roman Reloaded Tour in 2012 gathered more steam than her Pink Friday Tour in 2010. The Pink Friday Tour began on May 2012 and was scheduled to play over 40 shows in Europe, Asia, Australia and North America.

Despite its chart performance, "Starships" continued to generate a whirlwind of controversy for Nicki because of its zesty pop appeal.

Things became so heated the summer after the release of *Pink Friday: Roman Reloaded* that Lil Wayne withdrew her performance from Hot 97's Summer Jam after one of the radio station's DJs, Peter Rosenberg, attacked the song and its fans.

"It was an awkward, unfortunate exchange between hip-hop's competing poles of traditionalism and experimentation," Jon Caramanica wrote in the New York Times. "It was even more awkward because, more so than almost any other current rapper, Ms. Minaj can operate successfully at both extremes—she's a top-notch rapper when she chooses to be and a flagrant rewirer of hip-hop orthodoxies much of the rest of the time. Her liminal status was what was really on trial. "Starships" was just a sacrificial jam. Lil Wayne came to her rescue."

Her hypeman/boyfriend, Safaree Lloyd Samuels, known by various names such as SB, Scaff Beezy, VVS Beezy, and Scaff Breezy, took to Twitter to defend her against Rosenberg. Samuels is the

Co-executive producer and A&R coordinator of *Pink Friday: Roman Reloaded*. He is also rumored to be her fiancé.

"YOOO PETER ROSENBURG WHEN I COME TO SUMMA JAM YOU GETTING PUNCHED IN YA F*CKING FACE U F*CKING P*SSY!!!!!!! I PROMISE U N*GGA!!!!!" Samuels tweeted.

Rosenberg responded with force, YoRaps reports. He took to the airwaves on Hot 97, saying that he will gladly meet Safaree face to face, and defending his criticism of the song.

"Nicki's boyfriend went on Twitter and said he was gonna punch me in the face because I don't like a pop dance song that his girlfriend made. Word homie? That's your favorite song? Is that your favorite song? A girly a** dance pop song?" Rosenberg said.

"I'll tell you what Nicki's boyfriend, you want to punch me in the face because I don't like pop dance songs? Please go right ahead. Yeah, and make that check payable to Peter E. Rosenberg. I got you! I got you! [You gonna sue?] Absolutely!"

No matter. Nicki Minaj has made pop chart history, by becoming the first singer to have 21 consecutive weeks in the top 10 for "Starship", according to Starzlife.

"Starships" surpassed the Black Eyed Peas' 2009 single "I Gotta Feeling", which spent 20 weeks in the top 10, the site reports.

Recognizing a talent, it would seem fitting that Will.i.am would rise to Nicki's defense.

"I'm proud of Nicki," Will.i.am said, according to Colin Daniels of Digital Spy. "You can't listen to this stuff about not being real hip-hop. You gotta go and get it.

"Whatever the music is called that's what it's called whether it's hip-hop, pop, rock, gospel or a freaking musical, who cares? Nicki is an artist and she is expressing herself. Why limit yourself?

"Hip-hop was broadening itself in the '90s. You had A Tribe Called Quest and Death Row. You had Lauryn Hill singing and rapping.

You had Too Short, Outkast, Nas and the Roots. Hip-hop was broadening itself.

"Now hip-hop is limiting itself. If hip-hop is going to continue to limit people I say, 'f**k hip-hop'. It's like the most unhealthiest community.

"I want Nicki to continue to show the world what hip-hop can be. It doesn't have to always be about fucking this stripper girl or getting money," Will.i.am continued. "I would rather be interested to hear what Chuck D thinks than some blogger or radio host."

Still, the Rosenberg battle occurred in the midst of her world tour. After her brief hiatus away from Twitter in April, she returned with resolve to stay in touch with the Barbz. In fact, shortly after announcing her tour dates in North America, she tweeted back to fans who were unhappy their cities were not included on the tour. She explained that some cities that were not included were slated to receive radio appearances.

One of her first stops on the Roman Reloaded Tour was at a sold-out performance in Tokyo at the end of May. While the show received rave reviews, the big news occurred off stage.

MTV News reported: Nicki Minaj's Pink Friday Tour touched down in Tokyo, Japan, last week, and following one of the rapper's colorful stage shows, things took a devastating turn: One of Nicki's fans was murdered after attending the May 25 concert.

On Thursday (May 31), Nicki took to Twitter to send condolences and deny allegations that her dancer was involved in the incident.

"Saddened to learn one of my precious fans; found tragically murdered in Japan. My love & prayers are with the family of Nicola Furlong," Nicki wrote.

The 21-year-old fan, a foreign exchange student from Dublin City University in Ireland, was found dead in a Tokyo hotel room after attending Nicki's show at Zepp Tokyo a few hours earlier.

An early report on PerezHilton.com stated that Furlong and her friend Sarah Maher linked up with Nicki's backup dancer James Blackston and another musician, Larry Perry, after the show, heading to the men's hotel rooms.

Furlong was later found strangled to death in the room, while Maher reported that she was sexually assaulted by both men in a taxi.

After sending her condolences to the slain fan's family, Nicki addressed rumors that her dancer was involved, tweeting directly at the celebrity gossip blogger. "My dancers had nothing to do w/ this tragedy. No one in my entourage was questioned or arrested. They all flew home from Japan," she wrote. "That person on your [site] is NOT my dancer. We do NOT know the men in custody. Too much misleading information."

While the Summer Jam debacle occurred nearly a week after the bad news from Japan, the tour vastly improved after New York and Japan.

She did, however, catch flack for a chicken order after a performance at the Apollo in Manchester, England.

Ross McDonagh of the London Daily Mail said that she surprised staff in Nando's, a Portuguese-themed restaurant after she ordered £3,000 ($4,700) worth of their tasty take-away chicken all at once.

"According to the Daily Star, a source close to the singer claimed she ordered 550 chicken legs, 300 chicken wings and 60 bottles of coke, adding it was enough to fill 'a whole car'...A spokeswoman for Nando's restaurant confirmed Nicki is a fan. 'A lot of the US artists are fans of Nando's, like Rihanna,'"

A representative of the rapper said she probably had the order prearranged so she wouldn't miss closing time, McDonagh wrote.

"'The gig finished about 12 and she did a signing after the show," he wrote. "I can't imagine Nando's would have been open at that time. She was straight off back to America that night,' he said. 'She did a meet and greet thing after the show, and there was some after-party that she went to. But I wouldn't be surprised if she went to Nando's or had a big order from Nando's,' " he wrote.

Not unlike other artists, Nicki's tour rider has become fodder for the tabloids. She has been known to order scrambled egg whites, turkey bacon, toast, Belgian waffles, strawberries, assorted juices and a large fruit platter, according to the London Daily Mail. Lunch, the paper writes, can consist of buckets of spicy fried chicken - no thighs, a lot of wings - a large cheese platter, a deli tray filled with cold meats and a set of silverware to help shovel it all down.

No love lost. The Barbz knows that a gal has to eat. Most of all, they know about her love for fried chicken. After all, she wore it as a necklace on the red carpet! She also likes her dressing room to be laced up "like something of Aladdin," she told People magazine, saying she likes to be surrounded by bright, eclectic objects.

"[My dressing room] looks like something out of Aladdin," she told People magazine. "Pink flowers and candles, white rugs, couches covered in pink satin."

Indeed, her costumes are as unconventional as her dressing room.

"In the first act, I have three layers of clothes on. Then I just strip down as I go. I have about 100 wigs," she told People. She interacts with the crowd by showering them with enigmatic liquid.

"I have a big, colourful gun that I spray the audience with, I don't tell anyone what I'm spraying. It's a mystery!"

After performances, she said: "I eat olives with a towel on! No word on Nando's chicken!

Beyond that, Nicki continued to make tracks on the tour, especially in England. One reviewer described her style as a porn-star Pokémon persona seen through a sequence of lurid videos.

"Excepting the odd frozen moment of vocal eccentricity in an ultra-commercial four-to-the-floor stomper like "Starships", the tension between the two different strands of Nicki's endeavour (the visceral ardour of her rapping and the blandness of her pop hits) is never actually resolved in the music. But on tonight's evidence, it's not just the lady herself who considers such a resolution unnecessary,"

Ben Thompson wrote in the Telegraph:

"The same teenage fans obediently waving their hands in the air to sub-Katy Perry "Woah ooh!" choruses have also committed to the memory of her scabrously intricate mix-tape raps. Maybe it really is OK to like both," he continued.

On July 16, 2012, the North American part of the tour kicked off to a sold out show in Chicago.

Chicago Tribune music critic Greg Kot wrote in a review the following day that Nicki delivered a solid performance after a "mechanical run-through of some of the catchiest pop music of the last couple of years." The hits, from "Moment 4 Life" to "Starships," dominated the first part of the show, which was divided into three distinct portions, focusing on hip-hop, dance pop and ballads, he wrote.

"But two-thirds of the way into the concert, Nicki went off-script and reclaimed her turf," Kot continued. "She started rapping like the performer who "used to play in front of 200 people at a club," the precocious personality who caught the attention of rap king-maker Lil Wayne.

It saved the show."

After Chicago and several other dates, she roared to Southeast Asia, stopping in Manila. Over 12,000 Barbzs flocked to the SM Mall of Asia Arena to watch the superstar perform during her only Southeast Asian pit stop, Nicki Wang wrote in the *Manila Standard Today*. She said that fans dressed up in all shades of pink and were even imitating their idol's infamous eccentric 'do.

"You're going to be in my heart forever, this place reminds me so much of Trinidad," Wang wrote. "It's absolutely beautiful. Earlier when I look at the Manila Bay it reminded me of Trinidad," the singer said stirring the crowd to a hysterical frenzy.

Wang went on to say that "the very much willing audience danced, jumped up and down in their seats turning the concert venue into a big rave party, a mass shindig if you will, most especially when she performed "Starships" culled from her latest album, and the worldwide monster hit, 'Super Bass,'"

"Manila can you make some noise for yourself? You've been wonderful tonight," Wang wrote. "Did you guys come here to party?"

When she rode through Detroit in late-July with her wild energy, fans went crazy, according to the Detroit Free Press. She performed before a sold-out crowd at the Fox Theatre for 90-minutes, performing "Starships" and "Super Bass," throwing free t-shirts into the audience and cooling the crowd with a watergun.

- Charnae Sanders of the Detroit Free Press reports that fans said the following about her performance:

- Andrew Jackson, 22, of Hillman: "It was awesome. I loved everything. She did special effects and everything, it was unexpected."

- Victoria Charlie, 16, of Detroit: "I felt it was really amazing and when she sang 'Fire Burns,' it almost made me cry."

- Dexter Ray, 20, of Detroit: "I was up there with her and when I touched her, she made me feel like a superstar....I was jumping with a towel, she noticed it....She said we (were) the loudest crowd and I was proud to represent the 'D.'"

- April Jackson, 18, of Detroit: "The whole production was beautiful and colorful, every costume change showed her different styles and different sides of her personality from girly to hardcore....The only thing I was disappointed about the whole night was the high prices of the t-shirts and hoodies and the fact that our city name was forgotten on the list of tour dates."

- Ashley Grayson, 20, of Warren: "I loved it, it touched my soul...I loved when she sang "Fire Burns", because I can relate to the song because of a bad relationship."

- Ferlinda Anderson, 50s, of Ann Arbor: "It was great and very energetic. I danced the whole time I was there."

- Edwina Burckhardt, 14, of Royal Oak: "I thought it was really fun and I loved when she performed 'Super Bass.' "

- Mary Shirk, 17, of Bloomfield Hills: "I liked it, it's the best show I've ever been to....Her music is really good."

Meanwhile, during her tour, Nicki continued to make videos and release singles. In mid-July 2012, she released her fourth single and video for "Pound the Alarm" from *Roman Reloaded.*

For the Carnivale-like theme of her Trinidad-based music video, Nicki donned a plethora of feathers during an appearance on the Tonight Show on Friday (July 13).

"The late-night gig marked the first time Nicki did the song live (her US tour didn't kick off until later in the month) so she pulled out all the stops: tons of cleave, super hot backup dancers, and a sparkly nude bodysuit that looked as if it could've been stolen straight out of former tour mate Britney Spears' closet," Idolator wrote.

A bit of a scandal broke out when it was reported that she was allegedly cheated out of $100,000 by a local producer when she was shooting the "Pound the Alarm" video in her homeland Trinidad, according to Radaronline.

"Apparently, the producer took the cash and never completed the work he was appointed to do," Mstar reported. "The producer has countered the rumor and said that Nicki owes him money for the work that he did. He also complained about the negative press surrounding his company since this allegation came out."

But Nicki's indefatigable passion and drive continued to propel her to new heights. Indeed, her career was starting to mirror the lyrics of her popular hit, "Starships"; it was taking off like a Starship: "*Hands up, and touch the sky. Can't stop, 'cause we're so high. Let's do this one more time, Starships were meant to fly. Hands up, and touch the sky.*"

Roman Reloaded 2012 Tour Dates:

05-10 San Francisco, CA—Wild 94.9's Wild Jam

05-12 Los Angeles, CA—KIIS FM's Wango Tango

05-16 Sydney, Australia—Hordern Pavilion

05-18 Melbourne, Australia—Hisense Arena

05-22 Osaka, Japan—Namba Hatch

05-23 Tokyo, Japan—Zepp

05-25 Yokohoma, Japan—Yokohoma Bay Hall

06-01 Philadelphia, PA—Wired 96.5 Fest

06-02 Boston, MA—Jam'n 94.5 Summer Jam

06-03 New York, NY—Hot 97 Summer Jam

06-08 Stockholm, Sweden—Annexet

06-09 Oslo, Norway—Oslo Spektrum

06-11 Copenhagen, Denmark—Falkoner Theatre

06-13 Brussels, Belgium—Ancienne Beliguque

06-16 Berlin, Germany—Tempodrome06-18 Amsterdam, Netherlands—Heineken Music Hall

06-21 Milan, Italy—Alcatraz

06-24 London, England—Hammersmith Apollo

06-25 London, England—Hammersmith Apollo

06-26 Birmingham, England—NIA Birmingham

06-28 Manchester, England—Manchester Apollo

07-04 Dublin, Ireland—Olympia

07-06 Paris, France—Zenith

07-07 London, England—Wireless Festival

07-08 Balado, Scotland—T in the Park

07-16 Chicago, IL—The Chicago Theatre

07-17 Detroit, MI—Fox Theatre Detroit

07-19 Cleveland, OH—State Theatre at Playhouse Square

07-20 Hartford, CT—Hot Jam

07-22 Atlanta, GA—Fox Theatre Atlanta

07-24 Miami, FL—James L. Knight Center

07-26 Birmingham, AL—Boutwell Auditorium

07-28 Houston, TX—Bayou Music Center

07-29 Dallas, TX—Verizon Theatre at Grand Prairie

07-31 St. Louis, MO—Peabody Opera House

08-02 Denver, CO—Wells Fargo Theatre

08-04 Las Vegas, NV—Planet Hollywood Resort & Casino

08-07 Phoenix, AZ—Comerica Theatre

08-11 Seattle, WA—Paramount Theatre

08-12 Vancouver, Canada—Queen Elizabeth Theatre

08-18 Hylands Park and Weston Park, England—V Festival

Did it on 'em

Shitted on 'em, man I just shitted on 'em Shitted on 'em, p-p-put yo' number twos in the air if you did it on 'em Shitted on 'em, man I just shitted on 'em Shitted on 'em, p-p-put yo' number twos in the air if you did it on 'em.

All these bitches is my sons And I'ma go and get some bibs for 'em A couple formulas, little pretty lids on 'em If I had a dick, I would pull it out and piss on 'em

L-l-let me shake it off I just signed a couple deals, I might break you off And we ain't making up, I don't need a mediator Just let them bums blow steam, r-r-radiator

Shitted on 'em, man I just shitted on 'em Shitted on 'em, p-p-put yo' number twos in the air if you did it on 'em Shitted on 'em, man I just shitted on 'em Shitted on 'em, p-p-put yo' number twos in the air if you did it on 'em

This stone is flawless, F-f-f1 I keep shooters up top in the F1 A lot of bad bitches begging me to F1 But I'ma eat them rap bitches when the chef come

—Nicki Minaj

IX

BET, Boobs and the Bronx

The honors continued to roll in for Nicki. In July 2012, at the height of her Pink Friday: Roman Reloaded Tour, BET awarded her best female hip-hop artist. It was her third consecutive time taking the prize.

"I really, really appreciate BET for keeping this category alive, and I appreciate all the female rappers doing their thing, past, present and future," she said, before being censored for uttering profanity.

She also performed Champion. Backed by a string orchestra and surrounded with rings of fire and strobe lights, she rapped alongside 2 Chainz in front of a chorus of backup dancers.

"Tracking Nicki Minaj's wardrobe is like trying to follow her lyrics—you need a Red Bull and Nuvigil cocktail with a chaser just to keep up," wrote Leslie Gornstein of E.

"But we're gonna try anyway, just for you, even though she went through three changes that seemed like 14 different looks at the BET Awards the other night...for her on-stage performance, the rapper paired a black lace sock, which was then tugged and stretched over her entire torso, with a black tutu," she continued. "Then she took a break—at least, a break by her standards—with her gal-pal Kim Kardashian a set of gravity-defying black platform boots and a leather turtleneck.

"But by the time the "Beez in the Trap" singer was raking in awards she had changed yet again, this time into a getup that included (big breath here) a neon bra, painted-on snakeskin-print leggings by Ekaterina Kukhareva, a patchwork croc bolero and black Louboutin pumps.

Assuredly, Nicki had moved way past her mixtape warcry days of "It's Barbie, bitch!" With the flick of a pink wig and the wink of her long fake lashes, she has transfixed a nation with her crazy rhymes, crazy alter egos and wild style. She even has her own dedicated online encyclopedia, Wiki Minaj, which is dedicated to all things related to the artist.

Indeed, her brand continued to flourish. In fall 2012, she was scheduled to release a perfume and clothing line. She also has OPI's Nicki Minaj nail polish collection and recently signed a deal with Adidas designer Jeremy Scott for the Adidas Original Fall/Winter 2012 Collection. And Nicki, a.k.a. Roman, is slated to be the new face of a Pepsi beverage, nabbing a multi-million dollar deal.

She is a branding machine. The New York Times wrote in July 2012 that "it is an essential part of the star's arsenal, from her signature wigs, her unexpected and sometimes ludicrous fashion choices, to her endorsements. She is surface, and surface is her. But that surface obscures her innards to a degree matched in pop music only by Lady Gaga."

She became a force on the economic front, becoming the first female rapper to make the Forbes' Cash Kings List, earning an estimated $6.5 million in the year 2011.

"Making her debut at #15 on Cash Kings 2011, Nicki Minaj is snatching up more than personal achievements," Vibe wrote. "She's the first female rapper to ever grace the list earning $6.5 million in the past 365 sitting above B.o.B and Pitbull," Vibe wrote. "Another surprise millionaire newbie was Wiz Khalifa who landed at numero eleven raking in $11 million this year."

She also expanded her brand to the big screen. Teen magazine interviewed her on her role as the voice of the adorable mammoth Steffie in Ice Age: Continental Drift! They asked what it was like for her to view the movie.

"It was fun! It was funny and heartwarming," she responded in a Q&A. " It was very, very intense in 3D. The teeth, jaws, and paws of the animals felt like they were right there in your face. But it was fun. I had a great experience.

When asked what it was like to play a wooly mammoth in the movie, she said she was excited and surprised. In a nod to her alter ego, they said they couldn't see her as that kind of animal.

"I was more excited than surprised," she said. "I didn't care what they wanted me to play; I was definitely going to play it. I'm really, really honored to be a part of the movie. Even with just a small role, I'm honored and excited to be a part of something that's been around for such a long time. I mean, this is the fourth installment, so it was a big deal for me. I think my character is pretty cool. She has a little flower in her hair. She is a mammoth, but she's a beautiful mammoth".

"In the movie, he's kind of the popular guy and I'm kind of the popular girl, and I secretly have a little crush on him," she told Teen. "I'm kind of like the loud mouth that tries to prevent him from liking another mammoth in the movie."

The 20th Century Fox film was a runaway success at the box office. The fourth installment of the studio's animated "Ice Age" franchise debuted in the No. 1 spot at the box office in July 2012. While it was the only film to hit the theaters, it opened with a solid domestic sum of $46 million, according to estimate from Fox.

"#IceAge4 Continental Drift is everywhere today!!!! :)," Nicki tweeted July 13th. Drake also commented about the release: "ICE AGE 4 today!! Can't wait to see it. I feel like I gave my mammoth a silky Leon Phelps voice. Enjoy kids," he tweeted July 13th.

The film definitely exposed Nicki to a younger generation and their parents and cleared the path for her to become an even bigger name in the annuls of hip hop, known as an all boys club.

But Nicki's road to success has not been entirely paved in gold and her gilded sexual panache has gotten her into trouble on more than one occasion. She endured harsh criticism, following so-called nipple gate or a wardrobe malfunction on Good Morning America in August 2011.

The Associated Press reported: "ABC News is apologizing for a wardrobe malfunction that gave singer Nicki Minaj more exposure than she bargained for. Nicki appeared Friday on the "Good Morning America" concert series, wearing a loose-fitting halter top that she occasionally had to adjust. As Nicki sang "Where Dem Girls At," some slips made one of her nipples fleetingly visible. Despite a five-second delay, the slips were seen during the East Coast's live telecast. ABC said they were edited out of Friday's later feeds to other parts of the country."

ABC said in a statement: "We are sorry that this occurred."

Given her trademark practice for signing boobs, questions arose about whether the platinum-selling rapper's nipple exposure was truly accidental. But the nipple gate storm quickly blew over.

As for her boob signing, it's a mainstay in her act and it's popular among the Barbz.

She is quoted as saying: "I think boobs are very empowering—and signing them is even more empowering…I've been doing it for years. Wherever I go, I sign boobs."

Nicki, according to Contact Music, will even sign men's chests if they want and finds it "funny" if the guys aren't in shape and have "moobs" —male breasts.

Despite its overtones, her propensity for boob signing does not mean she's a lesbian. When she hit the scene in 2009, there were rumors abound about her sexuality.

"On her 2009 mixtape, Beam Me Up Scott, she had songs like "Girls Kissing Girls," in which the first verse from Gucci Mane raps that you should beware of lesbians and bisexual women around your girlfriend," Natalie Stein wrote in a post at Bitch Media. In "Still I Rise," she talks about haters spreading rumors about her, including: You know her last name Minaj, she a lesbian And she ain't neva comin' out, look at currency. And in "Go Hard", she says she 'only stops for pedestrians, or real real bad lesbian.' So, is Nicki Minaj gay? Maybe. Will she come out if she is? Probably not."

In 2010, she was rumored to have had had sex with Remy Ma. Both squashed it as lies.

"No, I'm not gay," Remy Ma said flat out in an interview.

"That's definitely not true," Nicki said when asked if she was bisexual, I guess some people are thrown off by me embracing gay culture. But I don't feel the need to explain that. Unless someone asks me a specific question."

She plans to be married with children in 2022, she told Complex Magazine in March 2012. She prefers a boy and does not feel like she needs a girl, she said.

"Yeah, 'cause you think I'm going to dress her up in wigs, no. [Laughs] I really need a boy in my life. A baby boy. Because…I'm so attached to my little brother and I felt like that was my real son. And boys, they're just so, I don't know… My heart just melts when I see them."

Nicki doesn't envision herself rapping in 2022.

"I always said There's no way I could still be doing rap, cause what will I still be talking about? But now that the public has given me this opportunity to do all types of music, I might have more longevity. As long as I can continue to experiment, then I might be doing music in 10 years. I know that I don't feel like I need to be doing music in 10 years to feel fulfilled. And I don't want to be one of those people who doesn't know when to call it quits. Let's just say that".

She says that her heart will tell her when to call it quits.

"It's just about you and your heart, when you're still relevant to the culture. But who am I to know? I'm only on my second album. Maybe you never get that memo in your brain that tells you, Quit it. I would enjoy a career like Jay-Z's, where he raps because he wants to, not 'cause he has to. I think that's the scary part when, after 10 years in the game, people can't pay their bills and now you're desperate. And so that's why I always say, business first."

Like Beyonce' and Jay-Z, Nicki keeps her love life out of the spotlight though it's an open secret that she is dating Safaree, her so-called hypeman. But her make-believe world of paisley pink and purple mushroom clouds reportedly does not extend to her romantic life.

One such report allegedly occurred at the airport in Dallas in July 2011, according to the Dallas Observer, which obtained the official incident report that names Samuels as the unidentified man in an attack involving a suitcase to the case the face.

The Dallas Observer reports: "Minaj and a 28-year-old black male by the name of Safaree Samuels were involved in an argument at the Hotel Palomar's pool. Later, they returned to Nicki's room, where the two were staying together. There, the argument continued, at which point Samuels apparently decided to leave, taking with him a suitcase that belonged to Nicki but that contained personal belongings of his. When Nicki protested, Samuels picked up the suitcase and "shoved it across [Nicki's] chin and lower lip.

"Samuels then left the scene and did not return. At that point, a hotel employee called the police and fire department at Nicki's request, and, upon their arrival, Nicki was treated for bleeding on the inside of her lower lip. She declined to file charges against Samuels who has still not been found."

No charges were filed, but both took to Twitter to squash the rumors.

Safaree tweeted: "The general public are some stupid mutha-fuckas!!!! Y'all dicks believe anything on a website…. It's really a shame… Wut up tho Dallas?!!"

Nicki followed up, saying: "The fact that u believe a man either slapped or punched me in the face & didn't leave on a stretcher w/his balls hangin off? #getaF%cknLife"

If she is involved in a violent relationship, perhaps it was unavoidable, given the history of violence she experienced in her household, growing up as a child.

Her mother, Carol Maraj, said in a July 2012 interview with the Trinidad & Tobago Express that she tried to shield her children from the violence as much as possible.

"My strength came from my children, my hope, and my reason for living," Maraj told Renée Cummings of the Trinidad & Tobago Express. "I couldn't give up. They kept me going. I decided enough was enough. I'm leaving and I'm not going back. I had to take care of me and live for me. But it took a long time before I reached to that place."

Maraj told Cummings that she, too, came from a violent household. She grew up in St. James, one of 11 children. She was No. 10. She recalled symptoms of mental illness in one of her siblings, saying that it may have been part of the reason for the chaos.

"When I was in high school, one day I came home and my 18-year-old brother was breaking up all the louvers in the windows," Maraj said. "He was destroying everything. There was a lot of trauma in the house…There was just a lot of trauma in my early teens because of his illness. I was often afraid for my life."

That fear followed her into adulthood and she began to see it as normal, a way of life, she said. Looking back, she should have known that her future husband had abusive tendencies, she recalled. But when she got married at 20, she moved from one violent household to another, Cummings wrote. She said she held jobs at the Ministry of Works, Long Circular, in St James and in Big Yard, Diego Martin, handling payroll. She also worked at the National Insurance Board (NIB) as an accounting clerk and at the National Commercial Bank (NCB) as a foreign exchange teller.

"If I only looked at someone it was an argument," Maraj said. "If we went out, I couldn't dance with anyone. If someone who knew me saw me out in the street and I spoke to that person, it was a big argument and curse out in the street. I didn't realized it then, those early signs of abuse. I was very young when the abuse started."

She thought she had a new lease on life when she obtained her Green Card, she told Cummings. "My dad filed for me," she said.

She arrived in the Bronx when she was just 24 and enrolled at Munroe College. Her husband arrived six months later after she petitioned for him. She told Cummings that she wanted to keep the family together and needed his support to help her raise their children in a new country. She recalled that he got a job at American Express. "At first, it was nice, very nice," she recalled. "He was cooking for me and doing a lot of nice things."

Meanwhile, Nicki and her brother were in St James, with her mother. "The children came a few years after," Maraj recalled. "They were in very good hands. My mom took good care of them."

She told Cummings that her father helped her buy her first house in Queens on 147th Street, off Rockaway Boulevard.

"There was a lot happening in that house," Maraj recalled. "I didn't know my husband was a crack addict. But one winter night, in December 1987, he went into a rage, he was demanding money, he was so angry, and I didn't have any money."

He may have turned to drugs to calm his inner demons. She described her husband's life as being less than a picnic. "His dad passed away when he was 14," she said. He had a lot of responsibilities because he had to care for five siblings. His mother put a lot of pressure on him and he was beaten for everything."

She told Cummings that she and her husband are separated. "A few years ago, he said he changed, and he wanted help. I still love him. But as a brother in Christ. We've been over for more than 10 years now."

Looking back, she tries hard to put the pieces together.

"When did all of this happen? How did all of this happen? I was a 27-year-old woman, working hard, trying to be happy in my own way and then this devastation just comes upon me," she said. "The neighbors are hearing. You have to hide your face and bend your head. God didn't make me for this. I kept telling myself *God didn't make you for this. God didn't create you for this.* I promised myself I wasn't going to give up until I made me right. When things fell apart I always looked for another door because I knew this wasn't in God's plan for me. I never stopped going to church. Even if my eyes were blood-shot red I was in church. I had to refill on God's grace because my life had run dry."

Looking at Maraj, it's clear where Minaj got her style. Maraj was dressed to the nines in designer high heels, make-up and lashes, Cummings wrote.

"She's wearing Claudia Pegus," Cummings wrote, describing Maraj. "The creation comes to life. Bound in luminous fabric, bronze sequins spiral tulle rosettes. The glimmer of its iridescent shine throws like a high voltage spotlight that follows Maraj wherever in the room she goes. She's radiating with energy. She's in Trinidad. She's home. She's herself. She's happy."

Maraj told Cummings that she doesn't like much media attention, but she wanted to talk to her.

She says Minaj's resemblance to her mother is striking.

"That face can't hide," says Karen Hunter, Maraj's longtime friend and publicist. Hunter teases her about being shy after all these years. "Maraj cuts her a sharp eye but comical look that says, 'Girl, please!'

"Nicki's success changed my life drastically," she said. "Her success gave me a new outlook on life. We were living in Jamaica, Queens, and Nicki was talking to me and telling me Lil' Wayne was interested in her music and paying her a lot of attention. I told her we just have to pray on it. That God wouldn't bring her this far and not see it through. I told her God was going to complete it. I prayed and then I told her it is done! When she called me with the news she was so excited. We were all blown away by her success."

That success has allowed her to finally take time for herself. "It took a lot to help me prepare my mind," she said. "But I realized that it was time to start following my dream. When Nicki got her break I didn't have to work so hard anymore. I was able to relax and take care of me. All those years, I was going through so much and still running to work, every day, from nine-to-five. Because of Nicki I was now able to focus on me."

Nicki didn't get her chops from out of nowhere. Her mother is a singer and songwriter. She told Cummings that she planned to drop a CD in summer 2012. She's also a playwright who writes drama presentations for her church, Life in its Poetic Form Ministries on Washington Avenue, in Brooklyn, she told Cummings.

"I had to heal and build back my strength so I started writing again," Maraj said. "I started spending more time writing about my life."

She's been working on an inspirational book. "A book that looks at what brought me here, to this new place," she said. She credits the older women of her church with propping her up on those days when she was really down. "Those older women came to my house and prayed for us," she said. "God sent some strong and inspirational women to help me stand up."

She's also using her newfound strength to help change the lives of battered women. She's also been doing a lot of motivational speaking, sharing her story with women in New York City through the Centre of Domestic Violence in Manhattan, Cummings wrote. But she also wants to help victims of domestic violence in her country.

"When I left for Trinidad, the head of my church asked me if I thought I was going to Trinidad on a vacation," she told Cummings. "She looked at me and said, 'Carol you are not going to Trinidad on a vacation. You are going on a mission.' "

To be sure, Maraj is on a mission. So is her daughter, who "did it on" all of her haters.

"Pound the Alarm"

Oh, oh, oh, come fill my glass up a little more
We 'bout to get up, and burn this floor
You know we getting hotter, and hotter
Sexy and hotter, let's shut it down

Yo, what I gotta do to show these girls that I own them
Some call me Nicki, and some call me roman
Skeeza, pleeza, I'm in Ibiza.
Giuseppe Zannotti my own sneaker
Sexy, sexy that's all I do
If you need a bad bitch
Let me call a few
Pumps on and them little mini skirts is out
I see some good girls, I'mma turn 'em out
Ok bottle, sip, bottle, guzzle
I'm a bad bitch, no muzzle, hey?
Bottle, sip, bottle, guzzle
I'm a bad bitch, no muzzle, let's go.

Music, makes me, high

Oh, oh, oh, come fill my glass up a little more
We 'bout to get up, and burn this floor
You know we getting hotter, and hotter
Sexy and hotter, let's shut it down

Pound the alarm!

I wanna do it for the night, night
So get me now, and knock this over
I wanna do it like you like, like
Come get me, baby we're not getting younger
I just want you tonight, night
Baby we won't do it for life

Music, makes me, high

—Nicki Minaj

X

Nicki Minaj Tops the Charts

As perhaps the brightest star on the pop, R&B and hip hop charts, Nicki Minaj is smart to look toward the future, especially with youth and energy on her side.

She released "Pound the Alarm", the fourth single from *Pink Friday Roman Reloaded* to great fanfare in July 2012. A video also accompanied the release, which was shot in her homeland. She received rave reviews for a performance on "The Tonight Show" with Jay Leno, fresh off the European leg of her tour, which was sold-out for the most part. If Europe was in the throes of a financial crisis, it wasn't apparent from her Barbz, who flocked to her performances.

"Accompanied by a gaggle of shirtless men, accessorized with peacock green feathers attached to her derriere, the pop/hip-hop starlet rapped her verses followed by singing the chorus," VH1's Bené Viera wrote of the Leno performance. "The electronic dance pop song is destined for the dance club scene where the rhythmic beat moves you to dance. Her energy was high as she performed quite a bit of choreography while giving her signature animated looks.

As always, Nicki was thrilling to watch. Shooting confetti from what looked like a personal paintball gun felt like she was metaphorically and literally spraying confetti all over the stage she had slayed."

Before hitting the stage, she chatted with Leno about her prestardom days, especially working as a waitress at Red Lobster, where customers used to "hate" her. She told the audience that she made over $500 a week at 19 years old, which afforded her a brand new BMW. "And she had one thing to beg of Red Lobster customers for the waiters' sake: stop ordering extra Cheddar Bay biscuits," Iyana Robertson reported in Vibe.

"They always want too much bread," she told Leno. "That's what bothered me. You guys, please, if you go to Red Lobster, stop ordering extra bread. We're so busy in the kitchen and it's like, the kitchen is hot, we're waiting for your orders, and have another table. And we go to the table thinking it's a big emergency and they're like: 'Can we have some more bread?'"

She also said that she tries to serve as a positive role model for her fans and said that Jada Pinkett-Smith is one of her role models. "I try to mold them, I always tell them to stay in school, I don't want them to grow up too quick" she said. "I don't want them to rush to grow up, I want them to take it easy because I think when I was younger I thought I was missing out on something," she said. "I always loved Jada Pinkett Smith and I still do because I had the pleasure to meet her and she just seems so well put together, mentally. Like every time I see her in interviews, she's always had this thing about her that made me feel inspired."

While she continued to garner some criticism for being too pop oriented, the song won rave reviews from some quarters.

"If she's not satisfying the urban crowd with stripped-back hip-hop numbers, she's causing raves with synth-loaded club anthems," Digital Spy wrote in a review. "As such, it's the latter that has garnered much of her recent mainstream success and new cut 'Pound The Alarm' looks set to continue that trend. "Oh, oh, oh, come fill my glass up a little more," Nicki chants over RedOne-helmed beats and an Ibiza-ready chorus. We'll admit that it's easy to spot the similarities with previous hit 'Starships', but as the classic phrase goes: If it ain't broke…"

Still, the syncopated club kid continues to rise. Despite her success, she told Complex Magazine's Miss Info in March 2012 that a lot of what she does comes naturally, including the wild faces and body animations.

None of it's rehearsed.

"No, I hate rehearsing," she said. "I never rehearse what I'm gonna do in a video. It's just that I have this love-hate relationship with the camera. I wanna please the camera so bad. The perfectionist in my brain is like, "You have to be on." I always want to feel like I gave everything my all and never, never, never exhibit laziness."

She says it was difficult for people in the industry to understand her personae when she first hit the scene.

"In the beginning people thought they knew who I was but they didn't," she said. "They tried to create something. Whenever I'm being me, the people love it. They connect with it. But whenever I find myself in a situation—prime example, during a photo shoot, if a photographer is telling me every little thing to do, I shut down. And you might as well kiss the photo shoot goodbye. I'm an artist in every motherfucking sense of the word. I work well with people who trust my instinct and understand that I am the marketer and promoter of the Nicki Minaj brand. This did not come overnight. This did not happen from a record company. No manager created this."

Nicki still has moments when she has to pinch herself to check to see if life is real.

"If I wasn't doing it, I wouldn't believe it's possible," she said. "I remember when I was working with Jay-Z. It was like, "Oh my God. Did I really just do a song with Jay?" I worked with Mariah and it wasn't commercially successful. But I had fun and I made a real friendship with her. It was, obviously, a life-changing moment for me. It does feel like every moment is getting bigger and bigger. Not only did I get a call to do a song with Madonna, but then I got a call to do a video with Madonna, and then—oh, by the way—you're going to do the Super Bowl with Madonna. This is not really happening."

While she's enjoying the ride, she said she does not take it for granted.

"I happen to be a pessimist, and maybe that's a good thing because I don't stop to smell the roses—which is not a good personal thing. I don't stop and enjoy those moments," she said. "I'm just [snaps fingers] on to the next. Always on to the next and never in the moment."

Despite talk of a gaggle of managers, she said she manages herself. But she didn't always know who she was as an artist.

"I knew who I was as a person," Nicki said. "My morals and everything, they're still the same. And then I took it upon myself to create this artist, Nicki Minaj. I wanted to do what a label cannot do. Now, labels are going to think they can re-create this. [Laughs.] But they can't."

She discussed how she has changed the game in such a short time as executives scramble to find the next Nicki Minaj. But she's not worried about being knocked off the shelf.

"When I first got in, doing freestyles and mixtapes, I did a song called "Still I Rise", I was talking about how so many women were pulling me down and ripping me apart. I said, 'Every time a door opens for me/That means you just got a better opportunity to do you/Better understand these labels look at numbers and statistics/ If I win, you win, it's just logistics.'

"So in order for my theory to be proven right, I have to open doors for women. The up-and-coming females who wanted to get in—when you guys are coming out and dissing me, and all that negativity....They saw me as a threat instead of seeing me as "she's going to open the door for us." I never came into what I'm doing dissing anyone.

I gave everyone their props and it's unfortunate that people felt intimidated and attacked me. Then it became a ripple effect. But now it's all love. My music is a way for me to have fun. Sometimes I'll say things and I'll laugh. But it's all love. I'm in a great place and I just wish everybody the best".

Nicki Minaj is living her life. As she says in Pound the Alarm, "Come get me, baby we're not getting younger."

She is looking toward the future as she tackles every opportunity that comes her way.

Pound the Alarm!

Conclusion
Nicki Minaj

"The hip-hop movement that coalesced in the Bronx during the 1970s has spread around the globe, colonizing not just music, but also art, sports, fashion and every other aspect of popular culture. This black American idiom has seeded so many variants—in Europe, Australia, Africa, Asia and the Middle East—that some historians of music no longer speak of a single hip-hop culture, but point to plural schools of hip-hop that have distinctive flavors.

Hip-hoppers abroad may be working the underground, producing trenchant political commentary or wielding verse in an actual revolution. But rap in the United States has been thoroughly commoditized and brought to heel by its corporate masters. Gone from most playlists are the high concept rappers in the mold of, say, Mos Def, who once had wide exposure speaking to issues of the moment.

With some interesting exceptions, the medium is recycling well-worn ideas, as though the practitioners have reached a kind of creative limit. The rap video, which has long teetered on the pornographic, remains an homage to conspicuous consumption, with rap celebrities like Rick Ross singing of self-aggrandizement, piles of money and insanely expensive cars—just as any number of artists did in the 1990s.

The idiom has also remained overwhelmingly and unrelentingly male, with women mainly cast as part of the scenery.

In capitalism, everything that rises must converge, to quote Flannery O'Connor. Given that rap and pop are corporate products, it is only logical that they would coalesce. Mainstream pop stars are increasingly seeking street cred by featuring rappers on their records. Money talks, of course. And rappers known for hard-core lyrics clean up very nicely when they sign on for cameo appearances with fresh-scrubbed pop stars like Justin Bieber.

It was only a matter of time before a hip-hop star would blow through the lines separating pop from rap and appeal to two lucrative audiences at once. And it was as inevitable that hip-hop purists would swiftly cry foul. It is particularly upsetting to the hip-hop boys club that the most successful transgressor, a freshly minted megastar named Nicki Minaj, is a woman.

It is too early to tell whether she has the creative power to show a way out of the current situation or open up a broader space in rap for women generally. But she has been difficult to miss, raking in music awards and posing on magazine covers in the Day-Glo wigs and makeup that summon up Japanese anime.

She raps in hyperspeed in British, Caribbean and New York accents, and channels her engaging zaniness through alter egos, one known as Harajuku Barbie. She refers to the young girls among her fans as Barbs.

She is as much actor as musician, hopscotching among genres and personas more easily than most of her rivals. Look back at her earliest music video appearances, and you get the sense that she is driven to shed one role for another, maybe just to fend off boredom.

Her rise has been breathtakingly swift, even by Warholian standards. First came several guest appearances on chart-busting records by other artists. Then came her now legendary display in the 2010 video "Monster," where she appeared as a black-clad, heavy-rapping vampire engaged in a musical dialogue with a pink-haired, Barbie-doll version of herself. For pyrotechnics and complexity of verses, she outclassed her two heavyweight collaborators, Kanye West and Jay-Z.

"Two albums later Pink Friday and Pink Friday: Roman Reloaded and she is already being hailed, with some justification, as the most influential female rapper of all time."

—Brent Staples, The New York Times

Studio Albums/Singles

Pink Friday

—Released: 2010

—Chart Positions: #1 U.S.

—RIAA certification: Platinum, Gold

—Worldwide sales: More than 2 million worldwide

—Singles: "Your Love," "Right Thru Me,'" "Moment 4 Life," "Roman's Revenge," "Did it On'em," "Girls Fall Like Dominoes" "Super Bass," "Fly"

Pink Friday: Roman Reloaded

—Released: 2012—Chart Positions: #1 U.S.

—RIAA certification: Platinum, Gold

—Worldwide sales: More than 500,000 worldwide

—Singles: "Roman Holiday," "Stupid Hoe," "Starships," "Right By My Side," "Beez in the Trap," "Pound the Alarm"

Nicki Minaj Collaborations
November 2004: "Don't Mess With" by The Hood$tars

September 2008: "Ucci Ucci" by Enur

December 2008: "Lollipop Luxury" by Jeffree Star

June 2009: "Lookin' at Me" by Pearl Future

September 2009: "Ponytail" by Mya

November 2009: "Grindin' Making Money" by Birdman

December 2009: "Sex In Crazy Places" by Gucci Mane

December 2009: "Shakin' It 4 Daddy" by Robin Thicke

December 2009: "20 Dollars Remix" by Ron Browz,

February 2010: "Up Out My Face" by Mariah Carey

February 2010: "In My Head (Remix)" by Jason Derulo

February 2010: "My Chick Bad" by Ludacris

March 2010: "Lil Freak" by Usher

March 2010: "Get It All" by Sean Garrett

March 2010: "Coca Cola" by Gucci Mane

May 2010: "Dang A Lang" by Trina

May 2010: "Woohoo" by Christina Aguilera

June 2010: "Hello Good Morning (Remix)" by Diddy-Dirty Money

June 2010: "All I Do Is Win (Remix)" by DJ Khaled

June 2010: "Up All Night" by Drake

July 2010: "Bottoms Up" by Trey Songz

August 2010: "2012 (It Ain't the End)" by Jay Sean

August 2010: "Letting Go (Dutty Love)" by Sean Kingston

September 2010: "YM Salute"/"What's Wrong With Them" by Lil Wayne

September 2010: "Haterade" by Gucci Mane

October 2010: "Monster" by Kanye West

November 2010: "Dark Fantasy" by Kanye West

December 2010: "I Ain't Thru" by Keyshia Cole

December 2010: "Raining Men" by Rihanna

January 2011: "The Creep" by The Lonely Island

March 2011: "Change Change" by Verbal

April 2011: "Till the World Ends (The Femme Fatale Remix)" by Britney Spears

May 2011: "Where Them Girls At" by David Guetta

September 2011: "Y.U. Mad" by Birdman

October 2011: "You the Boss" by Rick Ross

October 2011: "Dance (A$$) (Remix)" by Big Sean

October 2011: "Make Me Proud" by Drake

December 2011: "Turn Me On" by David Guetta

December 2011: "Fireball" by Willow Smith

About the Author

Chicago-based author Lynette Holloway is an online content provider, serving as associate managing editor at Diversity MBA Magazine, Midwest bureau chief for The Root, a contributor at NewsOne and Xinhua News Agency. The award-winning journalist is a former associate editor at Ebony magazine and staff writer at The New York Times, where she covered the music and radio industries. Her work has been featured in Essence, Uptown and People magazines. As a political analyst, she has appeared as a radio guest on WVON's Perri Small Show and WEAA's Michael Eric Dyson Show. She has a BA from Macalester College and studied at the University of Chicago.

ORDER FORM

WWW.AMBERBOOKS.COM

Fax Orders: 480-283-0991
Telephone Orders: 602-743-7211
Postal Orders: Send Checks & Money Orders Payable to:
   Amber Books
   1334 E. Chandler Blvd., Suite 5-D67, Phoenix, AZ 85048

Online Orders: E-mail: Amberbk@aol.com

____*Nicki Minaj: The Woman Who Stole the World*, ISBN #: 978-1-937269-30-2, $12.00
____*Eminem & The Detroit Rap Scene*, ISBN#: 978-1-937269-26-5, $15.00
____*Too Young to Die, Too Old to Live: The Amy Winehouse Story*, ISBN#: 978-1-937269-28-9, $15.00
____*Lady Gaga: Born to Be Free*, ISBN#: 978-1-937269-24-1, $15.00
____*Lil Wayne: An Unauthorized Biography*, ISBN#: 978-0-9824922-3-9, $15.00
____*Black Eyed Peas: Unauthorized Biography*, ISBN#: 978-0-9790976-4-5, $16.95
____*Red Hot Chili Peppers: In the Studio*, ISBN #: 978-0-9790976-5-2, $16.95
____*Dr. Dre In the Studio*, ISBN#: 0-9767735-5-4, $16.95
____*Kanye West in the Studio*, ISBN #: 0-9767735-6-2, $16.95
____*Tupac Shakur—(2Pac) In The Studio*, ISBN#: 0-9767735-0-3, $16.95
____*Jay-Z…and the Roc-A-Fella Dynasty*, ISBN#: 0-9749779-1-8, $16.95
____*Ready to Die: Notorious B.I.G.*, ISBN#: 0-9749779-3-4, $16.95
____*Suge Knight: The Rise, Fall, and Rise of Death Row Records*, ISBN#: 0-9702224-7-5, $21.95
____*50 Cent: No Holds Barred*, ISBN#: 0-9767735-2-X, $16.95
____*Aaliyah—An R&B Princess in Words and Pictures* , ISBN#: 0-9702224-3-2, $10.95
____*You Forgot About Dre: Dr. Dre & Eminem*, ISBN#: 0-9702224-9-1, $10.95
____*Michael Jackson: The King of Pop*, ISBN#: 0-9749779-0-X, $29.95

Name:_____

Company Name:_____

Address:_____

City:_____State: _____Zip:_____

Telephone: (____)_____E-mail: _____

For Bulk Rates Call: 602-743-7211   ORDER NOW

Eminem	$15.00	❏ Check ❏ Money Order ❏ Cashiers Check
The Amy Winehouse Story	$15.00	❏ Credit Card: ❏ MC ❏ Visa ❏ Amex ❏ Discover
Lady Gaga	$15.00	
Nicki Minaj	$12.00	CC#_____
Lil Wayne: An Unauthorized Biography	$15.00	Expiration Date:_____
Black Eyed Peas	$16.95	
Red Hot Chili Peppers	$16.95	**Payable to: Amber Books**
Dr. Dre In the Studio	$16.95	Mail to: Amber Books
Kanye West	$16.95	1334 E. Chandler Blvd., Suite 5-D67
Tupac Shakur	$16.95	Phoenix, AZ 85048
Jay-Z…	$16.95	**Shipping:** $5.00. Allow 7 days for delivery.
Ready to Die: Notorious B.I.G.,	$16.95	
Suge Knight:	$21.95	**Total enclosed: $**_____
50 Cent: No Holds Barred,	$16.95	
Aaliyah—An R&B Princess	$10.95	
Dr. Dre & Eminem	$10.95	
Michael Jackson: The King of Pop	$29.95